Homemade Healthy Dog Food Cookbook

2 in 1 Guide with 150+ Fast, Easy, and Safe Meal and Treat Recipes for a Balanced Diet to Enhance your Pawed Partner's Longevity and Happiness

Nora Howland

Welcome, Pet Owner!

Thank you for choosing "Heartfelt Dog Training"! Your decision to embark on this journey with us is greatly appreciated, and we are excited to be a part of your and your dog's training adventure.

As a token of our gratitude, we've included a special bonus for you at the end of the book. Don't forget to check it out – it's our way of saying thanks and helping you further on your path to a happy, healthy dog.

Happy Reading,
Nora Howland

Contents

Introduction: Nourishing Your Best Friend, One Homemade Meal at a Time

Hello there, fellow pet parents and dog lovers! If you've picked up this book, it means you're interested in one of the most meaningful and rewarding endeavors you can undertake for your furry friend—providing them with nutritious, homemade meals. First off, give yourself a pat on the back for taking this step toward a healthier and happier life for your dog. You're not just a pet owner; you're a caring guardian who wants nothing but the best for your canine companion. And believe it or not, this journey you're about to embark on is not just about food; it's about love, wellness, and the joy of sharing your life with a pet who gives you their unconditional love every single day.

Why Homemade Dog Food?

Now you might be asking yourself, "Why should I make my own dog food when there are so many commercial options available?" That's a fair question, and it's one many of us have asked before diving into the homemade food scene. The reality is that while many high-quality commercial dog foods are available, creating meals for your pup at home allows you to control every single ingredient that goes into their bowl. It's about knowing the source of their protein, the quality of their vegetables, and the absence of artificial additives or preservatives. Plus, let's face it: nothing says love quite like a home-cooked meal.

A Journey of Wellness

Another compelling reason to switch to homemade meals is the potential health benefits for your dog. Just as humans thrive on a balanced, varied diet rich in nutrients, so do our dogs. Commercial pet food, even the high-quality stuff, often lacks the nutritional variety that comes from whole, fresh ingredients. Additionally, some dogs suffer from allergies, food sensitivities, or specific health conditions that can be managed or even alleviated through a carefully curated diet. In this book, we'll discuss how to create meal plans tailored to various needs—whether it's age, health condition, or even pickiness. Yes, even the most finicky eaters can be won over with delicious, nutritious food!

What You'll Learn

In the coming chapters, we'll delve deep into the world of dog nutrition. We'll begin with the basics, exploring the key components that should form the foundation of any balanced canine diet: proteins, fats, carbohydrates, vitamins, minerals, and the often-overlooked component—water. From there, we'll move on to the practicalities of switching your dog to a homemade diet. The transition might seem daunting at first, but don't worry—we'll guide you through it step by step, tackling common challenges and offering solutions along the way.

Next, we'll explore how to make homemade dog food a sustainable, long-term option. Shopping, meal prepping, and cooking will become second nature as we share tips and tricks for simplifying the process without sacrificing quality. And for those days when life gets in the way—because it inevitably does—we'll offer quick and easy recipes to ensure your pup still gets a nutritious meal.

We'll also cover special circumstances, from cooking for dogs with allergies to adapting recipes based on size and age. Because let's face it, a teacup Chihuahua and a full-grown Great Dane have vastly different nutritional needs!

Safety First

While the focus is on providing wholesome, nutritious meals, it's essential to be aware of foods that should never make it into your dog's bowl. We'll highlight the "no-go" items—foods that are toxic to dogs—and discuss how to recognize signs of nutritional imbalances, so you know when it's time to consult a vet or a pet nutritionist.

Beyond the Bowl

Lastly, we'll take a holistic look at your dog's wellness, discussing how to monitor your pet's health, what changes to look out for, and how to adapt when health conditions arise. Nutrition is a powerful tool, but it's just one piece of the puzzle when it comes to your dog's overall well-being.

You're Not Alone

While the idea of cooking for your dog might seem overwhelming at first, remember: you're not alone. This book is designed to be your friendly guide through this rewarding journey, offering practical advice, and delicious recipes your dog will love. It's about nourishing your best friend, one homemade meal at a time, and relishing the tail wags, happy dances, and contented snores that are sure to follow.

So, are you ready to put on that apron and make some doggy "soul food"? Great! Let's get started.

Paws and spoons at the ready—our adventure into the world of homemade dog food starts now!

Part One - The Ultimate Guide

Chapter One

The ABCs of Canine Nutrition

1.1 Proteins: The Building Blocks of Your Dog's Diet

If you're diving into the world of homemade dog food, then you've made a wonderful choice for your four-legged companion. Just like us, dogs need a balanced diet to be at their best, and protein plays an essential role in achieving that balance. Think of protein as the building blocks of your dog's health, essentially laying the foundation for strong muscles, proper growth, and overall well-being.

Now, you may be asking, "Where do I start?" Well, protein is found in a variety of sources—animal and plant-based alike. Chicken, beef, turkey, and fish are all popular animal protein choices that you might already have in your kitchen. If you're looking to go beyond meat, eggs are another fantastic option! But don't toss the yolk; it's rich in nutrients and makes for a more wholesome meal. If your furry friend is more into plant-based foods or has specific allergies, don't worry. Lentils, chickpeas, and even quinoa offer protein and can be suitable substitutes for animal-based proteins in some cases.

The next big question is, "How much protein does my dog actually need?" It varies based on age, size, and lifestyle. Puppies, for example, require more protein for their growing bodies, as do active adult dogs who get lots of exercise. Older dogs might require less but still need a substantial amount to maintain muscle mass. A general guideline is to make sure protein makes up at least 18-25% of your adult dog's diet and around 22-32% for puppies. Always consult your vet for personalized advice tailored to your dog's specific needs.

Now, you might be tempted to go overboard with protein, but it's all about balance. Too much of it can lead to weight gain and kidney stress, while too little can result in muscle loss and lower immunity. The right amount of protein works in harmony with fats, carbohydrates, and other nutrients to make your dog's meal not just tasty but also nutritionally complete.

And let's not forget about quality. When picking protein sources, opt for lean, high-quality meats and plant-based options. Organic, free-range, and without any added hormones or antibiotics are ideal. It's tempting to use up leftover meats or offcuts, but fatty or heavily processed meats aren't the best choices for regular feeding.

In summary, proteins are the linchpin of your dog's diet. With the right sources and appropriate amounts, you're setting the stage for a happier, healthier pup. So go ahead, get creative in the kitchen and start cooking up some protein-packed meals your dog will woof down in no time!

1.2 Fats: A Concentrated Energy Source

Now that we've delved into the importance of proteins, let's shift our focus to another essential nutrient in your dog's diet—fats. Before you raise an eyebrow, let's clear up some misconceptions. Fats have gotten a bad rap over the years, but they are actually a concentrated source of energy that's vital for a variety of bodily functions. From supporting cell growth to aiding in the absorption of certain vitamins, fats serve several crucial roles that shouldn't be overlooked.

First, let's talk about the types of fats. You might be familiar with terms like "saturated" and "unsaturated" fats from your own dietary considerations, and these categories are also relevant for your canine companion. Unsaturated fats, which are usually liquid at room temperature, are generally better for your dog. Sources include fish oils, flaxseed, and certain vegetable oils like olive oil. Saturated fats, often solid at room temperature, can be found in animal products like meat and dairy. While saturated fats aren't necessarily harmful in moderation, an excess can lead to obesity and other health issues.

Omega fatty acids are another category you'll want to know about. Omega-3 and Omega-6 fatty acids, commonly found in fish oils, flaxseed, and some meats, are important for skin and coat health, immune function, and overall well-being. However, the ratio matters. Too much Omega-6 can lead to inflammation, so it's a good idea to balance these fatty acids in your dog's diet.

So, how much fat does your dog need? The general guideline for adult dogs is around 10-15% fat content in their diet, while puppies may require a bit more for healthy development, generally around 17-25%. Again, it's always best to consult your veterinarian for a tailored feeding plan, especially if your dog has special needs or health issues.

Quality matters when it comes to fats. Just as you would choose high-quality proteins, go for top-notch fats. This means avoiding fried foods or those high in trans fats, as well as steering clear of heavily processed oils.

A word of caution: while fats are essential, they are also calorie dense. Adding too much fat can quickly lead to weight gain, with the associated risks of obesity, including diabetes and joint issues. Be mindful of portions and balance fat intake with other nutrients for a rounded, wholesome diet.

In essence, fats are more than just a tasty addition to your dog's meal; they are a concentrated source of energy and essential for various bodily functions. So don't shy away from incorporating healthy fats into your homemade dog food recipes. They'll not only make the meals more delicious but also provide the nutrients necessary for a long, happy life.

1.3 Carbohydrates: A Controversial Component

We've talked about the importance of proteins and fats, and now it's time to tackle a slightly more controversial topic—carbohydrates. Some pet parents are all in favor of them, while others view carbs as unnecessary fillers. The truth, as always, lies somewhere in between.

First off, it's essential to understand that not all carbohydrates are created equal. Carbs can be complex, like those found in whole grains, fruits, and vegetables, or simple, such as sugars and syrups. Complex carbohydrates offer more nutritional value and are a good source of fiber, which aids digestion and promotes gut health. On the other hand, simple carbs provide quick energy but can lead to spikes and crashes in blood sugar levels, much like they do in humans. Therefore, if you decide to include carbs in your dog's diet, opting for complex ones is generally a better choice.

Now, you might be wondering, "Do dogs even need carbohydrates?" Technically, dogs can survive without carbs because they can convert fats and proteins into energy. However, quality carbohydrates can offer additional benefits like fiber, minerals, and vitamins. Plus, let's face it, quality carbs can make the meal more appetizing for your pooch. Just make sure they don't crowd out essential proteins and fats.

The trick is in balance and moderation. Too many carbs can lead to obesity and other health issues. An acceptable range for most adult dogs lies between 20-30% of their overall diet, although the exact percentage can vary depending on your dog's specific health needs, activity levels, and age. Always consult your vet for a personalized dietary plan.

Another consideration is the source of carbohydrates. Brown rice, quinoa, sweet potatoes, and various fruits and vegetables are all good options. Always cook grains and starchy vegetables to make them more digestible for your dog. And don't forget to introduce any new foods gradually to avoid upsetting your pup's stomach.

Here's where things get a bit tricky. Some dogs may have grain allergies or sensitivities. If that's the case for your furry friend, there are plenty of grain-free carbohydrate sources, like legumes and root vegetables, that can serve as alternatives. Just remember, each dog is different, so it may take a bit of experimentation and close monitoring to find out what works best for your specific pup.

In summary, carbohydrates may be a somewhat controversial component in your dog's diet, but they can provide additional nutrients and variety when chosen and portioned wisely. After all, a balanced diet is key to a healthy, happy dog.

1.4 Vitamins and Minerals: Essential for Overall Health

We've covered proteins, fats, and carbohydrates so far, but our exploration of your dog's nutritional needs isn't complete without discussing the smaller, yet incredibly important, components: vitamins and minerals. These micronutrients play a critical role in maintaining not just your dog's physical health but also their metabolic and cellular functions. Even though they're required in smaller amounts compared to macronutrients like proteins and fats, skipping out on vitamins and minerals can lead to a range of health problems.

Let's start with vitamins. These organic compounds support a variety of bodily functions. For instance, Vitamin A is essential for vision and immune function, while B vitamins like B12 and folic acid help with metabolic processes. Vitamin D is crucial for bone health, and Vitamin E acts as a potent antioxidant. While many of these vitamins are naturally found in quality protein sources, fruits, and vegetables, you'll want to ensure your homemade dog food provides a balanced spectrum. Sometimes, this might mean supplementing with a multivitamin designed for dogs, especially if you're not using a wide range of ingredients.

Minerals like calcium, phosphorus, potassium, and magnesium also deserve a spot in your pet's bowl. These elements are fundamental for bone health, nerve function, and a variety of enzymatic reactions within the body. For example, calcium and phosphorus work hand-in-hand to strengthen your dog's bones and teeth. Zinc supports skin and coat health, while magnesium helps with muscle and nerve functions. Many of these minerals can be found in meats, bones, and vegetables. But remember, balance is key. Too much of one mineral can inhibit the absorption of others.

The challenge with homemade diets often lies in ensuring that these essential vitamins and minerals are present in the right quantities and ratios. And this is where consultation with your vet or a pet nutritionist can be invaluable. They can help you fine-tune your recipes and may recommend specific supplements to fill in the gaps. After all, while cooking for your dog can be incredibly rewarding, it also carries the responsibility of meeting their complete nutritional needs.

It's worth mentioning that you should be cautious about using human supplements as a substitute for those designed for dogs. Certain vitamins and minerals are safe for humans in amounts that could be toxic for dogs. Always consult your vet before adding any new supplement to your dog's diet.

In summary, while vitamins and minerals may only be needed in small amounts, their impact on your dog's health is monumental. By paying attention to these micronutrients, you're taking another step toward ensuring that your furry friend lives a happy, healthy, and well-balanced life.

1.5 Water: The Overlooked Nutrient

There's one more nutrient that often gets overlooked, despite its immense importance: water. Yes, the simple, humble, and transparent liquid that makes up a large percentage of our planet—and our pets—is a cornerstone of any healthy diet. Though it doesn't contain calories, proteins, or any complex nutrients, water is the medium in which all biological processes take place. It's essential for digestion, nutrient absorption, and even temperature regulation.

Imagine a bowl full of the most nutritious, homemade dog food. It has the perfect balance of proteins, fats, and other nutrients, but without adequate water, the digestive system can't process these foods as effectively. That's right; water helps in breaking down food and transporting nutrients to where they need to go. It's the unsung hero that assists other nutrients in performing their roles efficiently.

The importance of water doesn't end at digestion. It also plays a crucial role in regulating your dog's body temperature. Dogs primarily release heat through panting, which relies on moisture from the tongue, mouth, and respiratory tract. In hot weather or after exercise, they must rehydrate to keep this cooling system functional. Plus, water supports joint health, aids in the circulation of blood, and helps with the removal of waste products from the body.

So how much water does your dog need? A general rule of thumb is that dogs require at least one ounce of water per pound of body weight per day. However, active dogs, lactating mothers, and puppies may need significantly more. And remember, if you're feeding your dog a diet primarily composed of dry food, additional water intake becomes even more important. Some pets also enjoy wet food or fresh fruits as a source of hydration, but these should never entirely replace clean, fresh water.

A constant supply of clean water is crucial. Make sure your dog has easy access to water bowls throughout the day, and if you're going out for a walk or a trip, take a portable water container. Be mindful of the signs of dehydration, which can include lethargy, dry gums, and a lack of skin elasticity. If you suspect your dog is dehydrated, consult your vet immediately.

In summary, water is an often overlooked but incredibly vital nutrient that plays an indispensable role in your dog's health. While we frequently focus on the complexities of proteins, fats, and carbohydrates, let's not forget this most basic, yet crucial, element. A well-hydrated dog is a thriving dog.

1.6 Toxins: Foods to Avoid for a Healthy Pooch

You're doing an excellent job diving into the wonderful world of homemade dog food. But while we're eagerly mixing, chopping, and cooking, it's crucial to remember that not all "human foods" are safe for our four-legged family members. Some ingredients might seem tasty and harmless to us but can actually be toxic to dogs. In this section, we're going to discuss some foods you should definitely keep out of your pup's dinner bowl.

Chocolate is a No-Go

Let's start with one most of us already know: chocolate. It contains substances called theobromine and caffeine, which are toxic to dogs (and cats!). Even a small amount can lead to symptoms ranging from vomiting and diarrhea to more severe complications like seizures and even death. So, keep those chocolate chip cookies for yourself!

Onion and Garlic Alert

Onions and garlic might be staple ingredients in many human dishes, but they're not suitable for dogs. They contain compounds that can damage a dog's red blood cells, leading to anemia if consumed in significant quantities. This includes all forms—raw, cooked, powdered, and so on.

Watch Out for Grapes and Raisins

The exact reason why grapes and raisins are toxic to dogs is still a mystery, but what we do know is they can lead to kidney failure in some pets. Just a small amount can be incredibly harmful, so keep the fruit bowl well out of reach.

Skip the Nuts, Especially Macadamia

Nuts like almonds, pecans, and walnuts can cause digestive upset and potentially pancreatitis due to their high-fat content. Macadamia nuts are especially toxic and can lead to symptoms like weakness, vomiting, and hyperthermia.

No Alcohol or Caffeine

It might sound amusing to share a "cold one" with your pup, but alcohol and caffeine are seriously bad news for dogs. Both can lead to rapid heart rate, hyperactivity, and even seizures. Stick to water or special dog-friendly beverages designed for canine consumption.

Xylitol is Extra Dangerous

This artificial sweetener is found in a variety of products, from sugar-free gum to certain brands of peanut butter. Ingesting even a small amount of xylitol can lead to insulin release, causing hypoglycemia (low blood sugar), seizures, and liver failure.

The Spicier, the Riskier

While some dogs might seem interested in spicy foods, ingredients like hot peppers can cause significant digestive upset. The capsaicin in peppers can lead to symptoms like diarrhea and vomiting, not to mention the discomfort your dog will feel.

Remember, when in doubt, always consult your vet or a trusted pet nutritionist to make sure that your homemade recipes are both tasty and safe. It's better to err on the side of caution to ensure that your furry family member stays in good health.

Chapter Two

Smooth Sailing - Transitioning Your Dog to a Homemade Diet

2.1 Making the Switch: Initial Steps

Now that you're armed with all this knowledge about what goes into a balanced, healthy diet for your dog, you might be eager to make the switch to homemade food. That's fantastic! But before you start whipping up gourmet meals in the kitchen, it's crucial to approach this transition in a mindful and gradual way. After all, sudden changes to a dog's diet can lead to digestive upset or even more serious issues. Here's how to make the switch smoothly and safely.

Consult Your Veterinarian

The first step, without a doubt, is to consult your veterinarian. They can provide tailored advice based on your dog's age, weight, health condition, and activity level. They may even recommend specific recipes or suggest tests to rule out any food allergies or sensitivities. Remember, each dog is unique, so a one-size-fits-all approach might not work.

Start with a Blend

Once you've consulted your vet, begin by adding a small amount of homemade food to your dog's regular commercial diet. A good rule of thumb is to replace about 10% of their regular food with homemade fare, then gradually increase this over a period of 7-10 days. Keep an eye out for any signs of digestive upset like diarrhea or vomiting and consult your vet if any such issues arise.

Track Reactions and Adjustments

Keep a food diary during this period, noting what you feed your dog and any reactions they have. This can help you identify any particular foods that don't agree with them or any positive changes you might not have otherwise noticed. Reactions can be immediate or may take a few days to appear. Adjust recipes and portions based on your dog's tolerance and nutritional needs.

Choose Simple Recipes at First

As you begin, opt for straightforward recipes that include a single source of high-quality protein and a limited range of vegetables or grains. This not only makes it easier to prepare the meals but also simplifies the process of identifying any foods that may not agree with your dog.

Transition Complete? Monitor and Maintain

Once you've successfully switched to a 100% homemade diet, it's vital to continue monitoring your dog's health. Regular veterinary check-ups are essential for ensuring that the homemade diet is meeting all of your dog's nutritional needs.

Making the switch to homemade dog food is a big step, but it's also an incredibly rewarding one. You'll know exactly what's going into your dog's meals, and likely enjoy the process of preparing them. Plus, there's something immensely satisfying about seeing your pet thoroughly enjoy the nutritious food you've lovingly prepared.

2.2 Monitoring Your Dog's Health During Transition

So, you've consulted your veterinarian and started introducing homemade food into your dog's diet. Excellent! The transition is an exciting time filled with culinary experiments and tail-wagging approval (or sometimes, disapproval). However, it's also a period that demands close attention to your dog's health. You're making a substantial change to what your pet eats, and even though you're doing it gradually and thoughtfully, it's essential to monitor how they're reacting every step of the way.

Physical Signs and Behavior

Keep an eye on your dog's physical appearance and behavior during the transition. A well-balanced diet should ideally result in a shiny coat, clear eyes, and a healthy weight. Energy levels should remain consistent or even improve. Note any changes, either positive or negative, as these can be important indicators of how well your dog is adjusting to the new diet.

Digestive Health

Any shift in diet can have immediate effects on your dog's digestive system. While some slight changes in stool consistency can be expected, persistent diarrhea, constipation, or signs of stomach upset are a red flag that the new diet isn't sitting well with your pup. These could be signs of food intolerances or just an indication that you're switching foods too quickly. In either case, consult your vet for guidance.

Weight Fluctuations

Homemade diets can vary in calorie content compared to commercial dog foods. So, it's important to monitor your dog's weight closely during the transition. Significant weight gain or loss should be discussed with your vet, as this may require portion adjustments or even a reevaluation of the entire diet plan.

Allergic Reactions

Be vigilant for signs of allergies, which can manifest as itchy skin, paw licking, or even ear infections. If you suspect a food allergy, consult your vet immediately. Identifying the specific allergen may require an elimination diet or other tests.

Regular Vet Check-ups

This might sound obvious, but frequent veterinary check-ups are invaluable during this period. Routine blood work, weight checks, and other assessments can provide a more nuanced understanding of how the new diet is impacting your dog's health.

Keep a Diary

Consider keeping a detailed diary during this transitional phase. Record what you're feeding your dog, including portion sizes, and note any changes you observe in their behavior, appearance, and health. This can be an incredibly useful resource for you and your vet, helping to pinpoint any potential issues or validate the success of your new culinary venture.

Monitoring your dog's health closely during the transition to homemade food will help ensure that your best efforts in the kitchen translate to the best health for your pet. So, stay observant, stay in touch with your vet, and adjust as needed.

2.3 Overcoming Common Transition Challenges

The journey to transitioning your dog to a homemade diet is filled with its share of joys and hiccups. While it's heartwarming to see your furry friend enjoy the food you've lovingly prepared, you may also encounter some bumps along the road. Don't fret—these challenges are completely normal, and there are straightforward solutions to most of them. Let's tackle some common issues you may face during the transition period.

Picky Eaters

Some dogs will gobble down anything you put in front of them, but others are more discerning—some might say fussy. If your dog turns up their nose at your homemade meals, try to introduce new foods mixed with their old favorites first. Gradually increase the proportion of homemade food while phasing out the old food. Sometimes, warming the food a little or adding a splash of low-sodium chicken broth can make it more appealing.

Digestive Upset

Switching to a new diet can sometimes lead to gastrointestinal issues like diarrhea or constipation. If this occurs, first ensure you're not transitioning too quickly. Reverting back to a smaller proportion of homemade food mixed with commercial food can help. If issues persist, consider consulting your vet for an adjustment in fiber content or other dietary components.

Nutritional Imbalances

While homemade diets allow you complete control over what your dog eats, they also come with the responsibility of ensuring a balanced diet. If you notice signs like a dull coat, low energy levels, or weight changes, consult your veterinarian. They may recommend specific nutrient supplements or adjustments to your recipes.

Time and Convenience

Preparing homemade dog food can be time-consuming, especially if you're not used to cooking often. Batch cooking can be a lifesaver. Dedicate one day a week to prepare all your dog's meals and freeze individual portions for convenience. Tools like slow cookers can also be a big help in making large quantities with minimal effort.

Cost Concerns

Quality ingredients can be pricey, and this might become a concern over time. One way to manage costs is to buy ingredients in bulk or opt for seasonal produce. Some vegetables and fruits that are beneficial for dogs tend to be more affordable in season and can be frozen for later use.

Sudden Allergies or Sensitivities

If you notice your dog scratching more than usual, or showing signs of discomfort after a meal, they may be developing an allergic reaction to a new ingredient. A vet consultation is essential in such cases, and you may need to conduct an elimination diet to determine the cause.

Remember, every dog is different, and what works for one may not work for another. The key to a successful transition lies in close observation, timely adjustments, and open communication with your veterinarian.

2.4 Making Homemade Food a Regular Routine

By now, you've ventured into the wonderful world of homemade dog food, navigated the transition, and overcome challenges. So, what's the next step? How do you make this newfound culinary practice a sustainable routine? After all, consistency is key when it comes to your dog's diet. Here are some tips for incorporating homemade dog food into your daily life in a manageable way.

Plan and Prep

A little planning goes a long way in making homemade dog food a part of your regular routine. Create a weekly or monthly meal plan for your dog, just like you might for your human family. Having a plan not only streamlines your grocery shopping but also helps ensure a balanced diet for your pet.

Batch Cooking

You likely don't have the time to cook every meal fresh each day, and that's perfectly okay. Many pet parents find that cooking in batches is the most efficient way to manage a homemade dog food routine. Spend a couple of hours on your day off cooking up large quantities of dog food, then portion it out into individual servings that can be frozen and easily thawed as needed.

Stock Up on Essentials

Some ingredients will become staples in your dog food recipes, like certain cuts of meat, vegetables, or grains. Buy these items in bulk to save time and money. Just make sure you have adequate storage space and remember to check the shelf life of each item.

Get the Family Involved

Making dog food doesn't have to be a one-person job. Involve other members of the family, including the kids, if they're old enough. Assign simple tasks like measuring ingredients or mixing, which can make the process quicker and more enjoyable.

Keep it Simple

While it's fun to prepare gourmet meals for your pet, remember that dogs have different taste preferences and nutritional needs than humans. Simple recipes are often easier to make and just as beneficial for your dog. You don't need to include a dozen different ingredients in every meal.

Invest in Quality Kitchen Tools

Good kitchen tools can make meal prep much more efficient. Consider investing in a quality food processor, a sturdy set of mixing bowls, and reliable storage containers that make portioning and freezing easier.

Schedule and Reminders

Last but not least, set a regular schedule for meal prep and feeding times. Use reminders on your phone or write them on your calendar to make sure you're staying on track. Consistency helps your pet understand when it's mealtime, and it also helps you maintain this new routine.

Incorporating homemade dog food into your regular routine may require some adjustments to your schedule and shopping habits, but the rewards are well worth it. You'll have the satisfaction of knowing exactly what your beloved pet is eating, and your dog will likely enjoy the varied, fresh flavors that homemade meals provide.

Chapter Three

The Art of Meal Prep for Pooches

3.1 Simplifying Your Shopping List

So, you're sold on the idea of homemade dog food, and you're ready to turn this commitment into a regular routine. Fantastic! But wait—before you dash off to the grocery store, let's talk about simplifying your shopping list. After all, stepping into the world of homemade dog food can initially feel overwhelming, especially when you're staring at a shopping list longer than your arm. Don't worry; we've got you covered with some tips to make your shopping trips easier, more efficient, and even cost-effective.

Core Ingredients

Every homemade dog food recipe will revolve around a few core ingredients—mainly protein sources and vegetables. Consider what proteins you want to introduce into your dog's diet; these could include chicken, turkey, beef, or fish. Then think about vegetables that offer good nutrition, like sweet potatoes, peas, or carrots. Stock up on these in larger quantities, if possible, as they'll be the backbone of many recipes.

Bulk Buys

Buying in bulk can be a cost-saving strategy, but only for items that you'll use frequently and that have a longer shelf life. Grains like rice or oats can be excellent bulk buys, as they're often used as a base in many dog food recipes. Frozen vegetables are another good option as they can be stored for an extended period.

Seasonal Shopping

Vegetables and fruits that are in season are usually fresher and cheaper. Seasonal produce can add variety to your dog's diet and can often be purchased in larger quantities and frozen for future use. However, remember to introduce any new fruits or veggies slowly to ensure they agree with your dog's stomach.

Local Sources

If you're lucky enough to live near a farmers' market, this could be a great way to get fresh, local produce and even meats at a reasonable price. Plus, you can talk directly to the vendors to understand how the food is grown or raised, which is an added bonus.

Plan and List

Before you hit the store, have a plan. Know what recipes you'll be making for the week or month and make a shopping list based on the ingredients you'll need. Organize the list by category (meats, vegetables, grains, etc.) to make your shopping trip more efficient.

Keep an Eye on Sales and Discounts

Grocery stores and online retailers frequently offer sales or discounts on bulk purchases. If you find a good deal on an ingredient you know you'll use often, and that has a good shelf life, don't hesitate to stock up.

Storage Solutions

Finally, make sure you have adequate storage solutions at home. You'll need a combination of refrigeration and freezer space, as well as airtight containers to keep dry goods fresh.

Simplifying your shopping list and being strategic about your purchases can make the entire process of making homemade dog food more manageable and enjoyable. With a little planning and organization, you'll become a pro in no time.

3.2 Mastering the Bulk Cooking Method

You've got your simplified shopping list in hand, and you're raring to dive into the kitchen. But let's be real—life is busy. Between work, family commitments, and spending quality time with your furry friend, you might wonder how you'll find time to cook every day. Enter the wonderful strategy of bulk cooking. It's the busy pet parent's secret weapon for keeping a consistent homemade dog food routine without spending hours in the kitchen daily. Let's break down how to master this time-saving method.

Choose the Right Recipes

When it comes to bulk cooking, not all recipes are created equal. Opt for meals that are easy to scale up and that will keep well either in the fridge for the short term or in the freezer for longer periods. Foods like stews, casseroles, and meat-and-veggie mixes are often good candidates for bulk preparation.

Gather Your Supplies

Before you begin your bulk cooking adventure, make sure you have all the necessary supplies. You'll need large pots and pans, a reliable set of cutting knives, measuring cups and spoons, and plenty of storage containers. Speaking of storage, ensure you have adequate freezer space to store the prepared meals.

Plan Your Cooking Day

Pick a day when you have a few uninterrupted hours to devote to cooking. Some people like to make this a weekend routine, while others prefer to use a weekday off. Whatever works for you is fine, as long as you can focus on cooking without distractions.

Assembly Line Style

Organize your ingredients and cooking utensils to create an efficient workflow. Cut all your veggies first, then move on to preparing your proteins. Cook your grains or other carb sources while your meat is simmering. The goal is to multitask effectively so that your cooking process is streamlined and efficient.

Portioning and Storing

Once all your dishes are prepared, it's time to portion them out. This step is crucial because it ensures that each meal you serve is nutritionally balanced. Use kitchen scales or measuring cups to get the portions right based on your dog's weight, age, and activity level. Then store these portions in individual airtight containers. Label each container with the date and contents to keep track easily.

Thawing and Serving

When you're ready to serve a homemade meal, simply take a portion out of the freezer the night before and let it thaw in the refrigerator. If you forget, most meals can also be thawed quickly in the microwave—just make sure the food reaches a safe temperature but isn't too hot for your pup.

And there you have it! Bulk cooking doesn't have to be a monumental task. With a little preparation and organization, you can make a week's (or even a month's) worth of meals in a single day. This ensures that your dog gets the nutritious, homemade food they deserve, without requiring you to become a full-time chef.

3.3 Incorporating Nutrient-Dense Foods

You're well on your way to becoming a homemade dog food aficionado, and now it's time to delve a little deeper into the realm of nutrition. After all, the ultimate goal is to create meals that are not only tasty but also jam-packed with nutrients your dog needs. So, how can you make sure you're squeezing the most nutritional value into every bite? The answer lies in incorporating nutrient-dense foods into your recipes. Let's explore this important concept.

What Are Nutrient-Dense Foods?

Nutrient-dense foods are those that provide a high level of nutrients relative to their calorie content. In simpler terms, they offer a lot of bang for your nutritional buck. For dogs, this could mean lean proteins that are rich in essential amino acids, fruits and vegetables loaded with vitamins and antioxidants, and whole grains or other complex carbohydrates that offer fiber and essential minerals.

Lean Proteins

High-quality proteins like chicken, turkey, and fish are excellent sources of essential amino acids that are vital for muscle development, cell repair, and overall health. Opt for lean cuts to ensure that you're getting maximum protein without the unnecessary saturated fats. Organ meats like liver can also be a nutrient-dense addition, providing a host of vitamins like vitamin A and various B vitamins. However, due to their high nutrient content, organ meats should be given in moderation.

Colorful Veggies

Vegetables like carrots, sweet potatoes, and green beans are excellent options. Carrots and sweet potatoes are rich in beta-carotene, which converts to vitamin A, essential for good vision and immune function. Green beans provide a good source of plant-based protein and are rich in dietary fiber.

Fruits in Moderation

Some fruits like blueberries and cranberries are packed with antioxidants and can be a healthy addition to your dog's diet. However, fruits also contain natural sugars, so they should be used sparingly. Always remember to remove any seeds or pits and consult your vet about which fruits are safe for your dog.

Whole Grains and Seeds

If your dog isn't sensitive to grains, whole grains like brown rice and quinoa can be excellent additions. They provide more nutrients and fiber compared to white rice or other processed grains. Chia seeds and flaxseeds are also nutrient-dense, offering omega-3 fatty acids and fiber.

Adding Healthy Fats

Don't forget about healthy fats like those found in fish, flaxseed, and olive oil. These fats offer essential fatty acids and are good for your dog's skin and coat.

Incorporating nutrient-dense foods into your homemade dog food recipes ensures that each meal is as beneficial for your pet as it is delicious. It may take a bit of research and label-reading initially, but once you've identified your go-to nutrient-rich foods, incorporating them will become second nature.

3.4 Making Quick and Easy Recipes for Busy Days

There are days when spending even an hour in the kitchen feels impossible. Between work commitments, family activities, and that ever-growing to-do list, we could all use a few shortcuts now and then. Don't worry, we've got your back! Here's how you can whip up quick and easy homemade meals for your furry friend, even on the busiest of days.

One-Pot Wonders

Who says cooking has to involve multiple pots and pans? One-pot meals are a lifesaver when you're short on time. Think stews or casseroles where you can toss in a protein, some veggies, and a carb source like rice or potatoes. Let it simmer while you tackle other chores. The result? A balanced, hearty meal with minimal kitchen mess.

Slow Cooker to the Rescue

If you own a slow cooker, you've already got a head start on easy cooking. Just add your ingredients in the morning, set the timer, and come home to a meal that's ready to serve. Chicken, sweet potatoes, and carrots make a great slow cooker combo, and you can even add a splash of apple cider vinegar for some extra nutrients.

Pre-Cut Veggies and Frozen Options

While fresh is best, there's no harm in taking a little help from pre-cut or frozen veggies. They're usually just as nutritious as their fresh counterparts and can save you a lot of prep time. Just make sure to check the labels for any added salt or preservatives.

Make Ahead and Freeze

When you do find the time to cook, consider making double or triple batches of your dog's favorite recipes. Portion them out and freeze them for future meals. On busy days, simply thaw and serve.

Repurpose Leftovers

Did you cook some lean meat and veggies for the family dinner? Make a dog-friendly version by setting aside some portions before you add sauces or seasonings that may not be pet-safe. Add some cooked rice or pasta, and you've got a quick meal for your pup.

Quick Mix-ins

For an ultra-fast meal solution, consider mixing some homemade components into high-quality commercial dog food. A spoonful of cooked chicken and a sprinkle of cooked carrots can elevate a basic kibble meal into something more nutritious and palatable.

Life moves fast, but that doesn't mean your dog's nutrition has to take a back seat. With a little creativity and planning, it's entirely possible to serve up quick, easy, and nutritious meals for your pet, even when you're racing against the clock.

3.5 Answering Your Meal Prep Queries

Meal prep for our four-legged family members is a relatively new concept for many, and it's natural to have a few queries, hesitations, or even little uncertainties. In this section, we're tackling some of the most common questions that you might have about preparing homemade meals for your dog.

How Long Will Homemade Dog Food Last in the Fridge?

Great question! Generally, homemade dog food can last about 3-5 days in the refrigerator. Of course, this depends on the ingredients used and how it's stored. Make sure you're using airtight containers to keep the food as fresh as possible.

Can I Freeze Homemade Dog Food?

Absolutely, freezing is an excellent way to extend the life of your homemade dog food. Portion the meals into individual servings, label them, and you can freeze them for up to three months. Just be sure to thaw the meals in the refrigerator rather than leaving them out at room temperature, which can invite bacteria.

Should I Cook Vegetables, or Can They Be Served Raw?

Cooking vegetables is generally recommended, especially for dogs who are not used to a diet rich in plant material. Cooking can make the veggies easier to digest and unlock certain nutrients. However, some veggies like carrots and cucumbers can be offered raw as a crunchy treat.

How Do I Know If I'm Giving My Dog the Right Portion Size?

Portion sizes can vary based on your dog's age, weight, and activity level. Your veterinarian can provide the most accurate advice tailored to your individual pet's needs. As a general rule of thumb, start by serving about 2-3% of your dog's body weight and adjust from there based on your dog's condition and energy level.

What If My Dog Has Allergies?

If your dog has known allergies or food sensitivities, it's crucial to tailor your homemade dog food recipes to avoid these ingredients. When in doubt, consult your vet for a comprehensive allergy test and personalized diet plan.

Can I Use Leftovers from My Meals?

Yes, but with some caveats. Human food often contains sauces, spices, and other ingredients that might not be safe for dogs. If you plan to share your meal with your pup, set aside a portion before adding any seasonings, sauces, or spices. Also, make sure that the foods you're sharing are dog-safe—no onions, garlic, grapes, or other toxic ingredients.

As you can see, meal prepping for your dog can be as simple or as detailed as you want it to be. The key is to tailor your approach to fit both your lifestyle and your dog's nutritional needs. And when in doubt, consult your vet for personalized advice.

Chapter Four

Tailoring Meals to Your Dog's Diet

4.1 Dietary Needs for Different Stages of Life

As we journey further into the world of homemade dog food, it's crucial to remember that our pups' nutritional needs aren't static. Just like humans, dogs require different nutrients at various stages of their lives. Puppies have different dietary requirements than adult dogs and senior dogs have their own unique needs as well. So, let's break it down and take a look at what you should be focusing on for dogs at different life stages.

Puppy Power

Ah, the joy and energy of puppies! They're growing rapidly and need a diet that supports this growth. Protein is the big headline here, required for the healthy development of tissues, muscles, and more. Essential fatty acids like DHA are also vital for brain development. However, keep in mind that too many calories and certain minerals in excess can cause growth-related issues in larger breeds. It's always best to consult your vet to tailor a balanced diet that promotes healthy growth for your puppy's specific breed and size.

Active Adults

Once your pup reaches adulthood, their dietary needs will stabilize somewhat. Protein remains important, but you might need to adjust the types and amounts depending on your dog's activity level. Highly active breeds might require more protein and fat for energy, while a couch potato dog might need fewer calories to prevent weight gain. Vegetables and fruits can be added in moderate amounts for fiber and essential vitamins.

The Golden Years

As dogs enter their senior years, their dietary needs start to shift again. They might become less active and require fewer calories to prevent weight gain, which could exacerbate arthritis and other age-related issues. Protein is still crucial but opt for easily digestible sources like lean meats. Adding omega-3 fatty acids can help with joint inflammation. Senior dogs can also benefit from fiber to aid in digestion.

Special Considerations: Pregnancy and Lactation

If you're caring for a pregnant or nursing dog, her nutritional needs will change dramatically. She'll require more protein, calcium, and other nutrients to support the growth and well-being of her puppies. Consult your vet for a comprehensive nutrition plan during this special stage of life.

Always Consult Your Vet

We can't stress this enough: For each stage of life and especially for transitions between them, consult your veterinarian. They can provide age-specific recommendations, offer insights into breed-specific needs, and help you navigate any health conditions your dog may have that affect their diet.

Understanding your dog's dietary needs at various stages of life will help you make informed decisions about their homemade meals. The right nutrition can significantly impact your dog's health, well-being, and even their lifespan. So, here's to happy, healthy eating for our four-legged family members, no matter their age!

4.2 Cooking for Dogs with Allergies

Let's talk about a topic that's becoming increasingly common: food allergies in dogs. It can be heart-wrenching to see your pup uncomfortable or even in pain due to allergic reactions. The good news is that making homemade dog food allows you to have complete control over the ingredients, making it much easier to manage food allergies. Let's dive into how you can tailor your homemade dog food recipes to meet the needs of a dog with allergies.

Identify the Allergen

The first step in cooking for a dog with allergies is identifying the specific allergen causing the problem. This usually involves an elimination diet, where potential allergens are removed from the diet one at a time until symptoms improve. Common allergens include beef, dairy, wheat, and chicken. Always consult your vet for proper diagnosis and guidance.

Choose Hypoallergenic Proteins

Once you know what to avoid, you can focus on hypoallergenic protein options like lamb, venison, or fish. These are generally easier to digest and less likely to trigger allergic reactions. However, make sure to introduce any new protein slowly and monitor your dog for any adverse reactions.

Opt for Easily Digestible Carbs

Carbohydrates like rice, potatoes, and oatmeal are generally well-tolerated by dogs with allergies. These are not only easy on the digestive system but also less likely to cause allergic reactions. Be cautious with wheat and corn, as these are common allergens for many dogs.

Incorporate Natural Supplements

Some natural supplements like fish oil or flaxseed can help manage the symptoms of allergies, thanks to their anti-inflammatory properties. Talk to your vet about which supplements might be beneficial for your dog and in what dosage.

Use Limited Ingredient Recipes

The simpler, the better when it comes to cooking for dogs with allergies. Limited ingredient recipes focus on a single protein and a single carbohydrate source, reducing the risk of encountering an allergen. These recipes also make it easier to pinpoint any potential allergens if your dog has a reaction.

Always Consult Your Vet

This can't be emphasized enough. Anytime you're dealing with health issues like allergies, it's crucial to consult your vet for a proper diagnosis and treatment plan. Your vet can help you choose the best ingredients for your dog and may also recommend tests to confirm allergies.

Navigating food allergies can be challenging, but homemade dog food offers a unique advantage in that you can customize meals to suit your pet's specific needs. With a little guidance from your vet and some careful meal planning, you can provide your allergic dog with meals that are not only safe but also delicious and nutritious.

4.3 Catering to Dogs with Specific Health Conditions

Now that we've covered the basics of homemade dog food and how it can cater to various life stages and even allergies, let's dig a little deeper into something many of us face: cooking for dogs with specific health conditions. Whether it's diabetes, kidney issues, or digestive problems, certain conditions require special dietary considerations. Let's explore how homemade dog food can help manage these issues.

For Diabetic Dogs

Dogs with diabetes need a diet that helps regulate their blood sugar levels. High-fiber, low-fat, and low-sugar foods are usually the way to go. Complex carbohydrates like whole grains or vegetables like sweet potatoes are often recommended as they release sugar slowly into the bloodstream. Proteins should be lean—think chicken or turkey. Always consult your vet for a tailored meal plan, as diabetic conditions can vary.

Kidney-Friendly Diet

For dogs with kidney issues, a low-protein and low-phosphorus diet is generally recommended. Less protein means less waste for the kidneys to filter. Fish, egg whites, and small amounts of poultry are usually more appropriate than red meat. Zucchini, squash, and bell peppers are examples of low-phosphorus vegetables that can be included.

Sensitive Stomachs

Dogs with digestive problems need foods that are easy on the stomach. Boiled rice and plain, lean meats like chicken are usually good starting points. Pumpkin is another excellent addition, as it can help regulate digestion, either firming up stools or aiding with constipation. When in doubt, simplicity is key.

Managing Weight

Obesity in dogs can lead to a host of other health problems, including diabetes and joint pain. A high-fiber, low-fat diet can help manage weight. Veggies like green beans can add bulk to meals without many calories, helping your dog feel full without adding weight.

Heart Health

If your dog has been diagnosed with a heart condition, a low-sodium diet will likely be recommended. Fresh meats like chicken, turkey, and fish are naturally lower in sodium than processed meats. Fresh fruits and vegetables are also low-sodium options but always check with your vet before adding any new foods to your dog's diet.

Always Collaborate with Your Vet

Whether it's a chronic condition or an age-related issue, your vet is your best resource for tailoring a diet to your dog's specific needs. They can provide detailed advice on what foods to include or avoid, and they may also recommend special supplements or medications.

Cooking for a dog with a health condition might require a bit more planning and consultation with your vet, but the rewards—a happier, healthier dog—are well worth the effort.

4.4 Adapting Recipes for Your Dog's Size

So far, we've been talking a lot about the kinds of foods you should be including in your dog's diet based on various factors like age, health conditions, and even allergies. But what about size? It's no secret that a Chihuahua has different nutritional needs than a Great Dane. In this section, we're going to dive into how you can adapt recipes to fit the size of your dog, ensuring they're getting just the right amount of nutrients without overdoing it (or underdoing it!).

Portion Sizes

First things first: portion size. It's the most straightforward adjustment you'll make based on your dog's size. Generally, the larger the dog, the larger the meal portion. But it's not just about doubling or tripling a recipe. Be mindful of caloric needs, especially since larger breeds can be prone to obesity if overfed. Consult your vet for precise guidance on how much your dog should be eating daily.

Protein Intake

Smaller dogs usually have faster metabolisms and may require a higher concentration of protein in their diets compared to larger breeds. That doesn't mean you should skimp on protein for bigger dogs; rather, it's about balance. Larger breeds may benefit from leaner cuts of meat, while smaller dogs might do well with richer protein sources.

Bone Size

If you're incorporating bones into your homemade dog food for added nutrients, make sure you're choosing bones that are appropriate for your dog's size. Large bones can be a choking hazard for smaller dogs, while small bones may not provide enough nutrients for larger breeds.

Veggies and Grains

The size of the vegetable or grain pieces in the dog food should also correlate with your dog's size. Smaller dogs may have a harder time digesting larger chunks of vegetables and grains, whereas larger dogs might not have a problem at all. Consider grating or finely chopping veggies for smaller breeds and leaving them in larger pieces for bigger dogs.

Caloric Density

Larger dogs often require foods that are less calorically dense to avoid unnecessary weight gain. On the other hand, small breeds that burn off energy quickly may benefit from more calorically dense foods. This could mean adding or reducing healthy fats like olive oil or flaxseed to your recipes.

Always Consult Your Vet

It's always a good idea to work with your vet to tailor your dog's diet to their specific needs. This is especially important when considering size, as different-sized dogs are prone to various health issues that can be managed or mitigated through diet.

Adapting recipes to your dog's size doesn't have to be a complicated affair. With a little bit of know-how and guidance from your vet, you can easily tailor any recipe to fit your pup, big or small.

4.5 Cooking for Picky Eaters

Now, let's address an issue that many of us face at some point: cooking for a dog that turns up their nose at almost everything. Yes, we're talking about those picky eaters who make mealtime a challenge. If your pooch seems more interested in sniffing around the kitchen than actually eating, this section is for you. Don't worry; even the fussiest of dogs can be persuaded to enjoy mealtime with a few strategic changes.

The Appeal Factor

Sometimes it's not what you serve but how you serve it. A warm meal can often be more inviting than a room-temperature one, so consider warming up your homemade dog food before serving. The heat can intensify the aromas, making the dish more appealing to your dog. But always double-check the temperature to make sure it's not too hot.

Go Lean on Proteins

Lean proteins like chicken or turkey can be more appealing to some picky eaters. The mild flavors and easy digestibility make these proteins a hit among many dogs. You can even poach the meat in a bit of chicken or bone broth for added flavor.

Mix it Up

A little variety can go a long way. If you always serve chicken and rice, try switching to beef and potatoes, or introduce a new vegetable into the mix. You can also rotate proteins and veggies to keep mealtime exciting. Just be cautious when introducing new ingredients; make sure to do it gradually to watch for any adverse reactions.

Texture Matters

Some dogs are picky not because of the flavor but because of the texture. Pay attention to whether your dog prefers chunkier meals or smoother, puréed options. Some dogs love a crunch, so adding a few diced vegetables could make the meal more exciting for them.

Make it a Treat

For extremely picky eaters, you can start by incorporating homemade food into their favorite treats or using it as a topper for their regular food. Once they realize that homemade food equals delicious food, you can gradually increase the ratio until they're fully transitioned.

Consult Your Vet

If your dog is exceptionally picky and refuses to eat entirely, it's crucial to consult your veterinarian to rule out any underlying health issues. Loss of appetite can sometimes be a sign of medical concerns that require immediate attention.

Being the parent of a picky eater can be frustrating, but remember, the goal is to ensure your dog is getting the nutrition they need to stay healthy. Sometimes it takes a bit of trial and error, but with patience, creativity, and perhaps a bit of culinary flair, you can win over even the most discerning of canine palates.

Chapter Five

Keeping an Eye on Your Pup's Health

5.1 Routine Health Checks: Your Pet's Report Card

You're doing an amazing job venturing into the world of homemade dog food. But while it's great to focus on what goes into your dog's bowl, it's equally important to keep an eye on how that diet is impacting their overall health. Think of routine health checks as your pet's report card—a way to ensure that all your efforts are leading to a healthier, happier pup. Let's take a look at what these routine checks might involve and why they're so important.

The Vet's Office

Regular vet visits are the cornerstone of any proactive pet healthcare plan. Just like humans get a physical, dogs need their check-ups too. Your vet will typically examine your dog's teeth, coat, eyes, and ears, and will also listen to their heart and lungs. Blood tests can provide additional insights into how well your dog's internal organs are functioning. If you've switched to a homemade diet, make sure to let your vet know so they can offer specific advice tailored to your pet's dietary needs.

At-Home Observations

Between vet visits, there's a lot you can do to monitor your dog's health. Pay attention to their energy levels, the condition of their coat and skin, and the consistency of their stools. If you notice anything unusual—like lethargy, flaky skin, or digestive issues—it might indicate that something's off balance in their diet, or it could be a sign of an underlying health issue that needs attention.

Weight Checks

Weight is another key metric to monitor. Overweight dogs face a host of health issues, including joint problems and a higher risk of chronic conditions like diabetes. Underweight dogs could be missing essential nutrients. Regular weigh-ins can help you gauge whether your homemade diet is providing the right caloric intake for your dog. Most vets have a scale available for public use, or you can purchase a pet scale for home use.

Dental Health

Good nutrition can have a big impact on dental health. A well-balanced, homemade diet can help reduce tartar build-up and improve gum health, but it's still important to regularly check your dog's teeth and gums. Dental issues can lead to other health problems if not addressed.

Keep a Health Journal

Consider keeping a journal or logbook detailing what you're feeding your dog, along with any health observations you make. This can be a valuable resource to share with your vet during check-ups and can help you track any changes or improvements in your pet's health over time.

Just like you'd report back to a teacher during parent-teacher conferences, your pet's health checks give you a chance to make sure everything's on track. These visits are a golden opportunity to discuss your homemade diet with a professional, make tweaks where needed, and celebrate the victories, however small they may be.

5.2 Recognizing Signs of Nutritional Imbalances

While the goal is to improve your dog's health through better nutrition, there might be instances where things don't go as smoothly as expected. Being able to recognize signs of nutritional imbalances is key to making timely corrections. So, what should you look out for?

Changes in Energy Levels

One of the first indicators that something might be amiss with your dog's diet is a noticeable change in energy levels. If your normally active dog suddenly becomes lethargic or your usually calm dog becomes hyperactive, it could point to a nutritional imbalance.

Coat and Skin Health

Your dog's coat is like a report card for their nutritional status. A dull, dry, or flaky coat can be a sign that your dog isn't getting enough essential fatty acids, for example. Conversely, a greasy coat could indicate an excess of certain fats in the diet. Pay close attention to their skin as well; issues like redness, itchiness, or hot spots can also point to nutritional imbalances.

Digestive Issues

Gastrointestinal upsets like diarrhea or constipation can sometimes be related to what your dog is eating. If these symptoms persist, it could be a sign that your homemade dog food might need some adjustments, or that a vet visit is in order.

Weight Changes

Unexpected weight loss or weight gain is often a clear sign that your dog's diet may not be balanced correctly. Too many calories or too little exercise can lead to weight gain, while a diet lacking in essential nutrients can result in weight loss. In either case, a consultation with your vet is advisable.

Bad Breath or Dental Issues

While bad breath can stem from dental issues, it can also indicate digestive problems or even a lack of certain nutrients. If dental cleanings and regular at-home care don't resolve the issue, you might want to look into your dog's diet as a possible cause.

Behavioral Changes

Believe it or not, your dog's diet can impact their behavior. Nutritional imbalances can lead to irritability, anxiety, or even signs of depression in dogs. While it's crucial to rule out other medical or environmental factors, food can indeed be a contributing issue.

If you notice any of these signs, your first step should be to consult your vet. They can help pinpoint the issue and may recommend specific tests to rule out other health concerns. Nutritional imbalances are generally fixable, especially with the flexibility that homemade dog food offers.

5.3 When to Consult a Vet or a Pet Nutritionist

Let's talk about when it's a good idea to call in the experts. While preparing your dog's meals at home gives you a lot of control over what they're eating, sometimes you might encounter questions or concerns that need professional input. So, when should you consult a vet or a pet nutritionist? Let's delve into some scenarios where their expertise can be invaluable.

Transitioning to a Homemade Diet

If you're just starting the transition from commercial dog food to a homemade diet, it's a great idea to consult with your vet or a certified pet nutritionist. They can provide guidance on the right mix of proteins, fats, and carbohydrates for your dog, along with any necessary vitamins and minerals to supplement.

Noticing Signs of Nutritional Imbalance

As we discussed in the previous section, signs like digestive issues, changes in weight, or an unhealthy coat can indicate a nutritional imbalance. These are definitely red flags that warrant a trip to the vet to rule out other health issues and to make any necessary adjustments to your pet's diet.

When Your Dog Has a Health Condition

If your dog has been diagnosed with a health condition like diabetes, kidney disease, or allergies, a homemade diet needs to be carefully planned to manage these issues effectively. Consult your vet for a treatment plan that incorporates dietary changes or work with a pet nutritionist who specializes in formulating diets for dogs with specific health conditions.

Age-Related Changes

As dogs age, their dietary needs change. Senior dogs may need fewer calories but more fiber and certain nutrients. Puppies, on the other hand, require diets high in protein and rich in certain nutrients for proper growth. Your vet can provide age-specific dietary guidelines to ensure your homemade meals are meeting your dog's needs.

Routine Check-Ups

Even if everything seems fine, routine veterinary check-ups should include a discussion of your dog's diet. Regular blood work and other tests can reveal deficiencies or excesses in certain nutrients before they become a problem, providing an opportunity to tweak your recipes accordingly.

When You're Unsure

Last but not least, if you're ever in doubt, it's always better to consult a professional. Whether it's uncertainty about a new ingredient, confusion over conflicting information, or simply a gut feeling that something's not right, don't hesitate to seek expert advice.

Consulting a vet or a pet nutritionist isn't an admission that you don't know what you're doing; rather, it's a sign that you're committed to providing the best care possible for your furry friend. Their expertise can complement your own efforts, ensuring that your dog's homemade diet is as nutritious and beneficial as it can be.

5.4 Adjusting the Diet Based on Health Changes

By now, you're well-versed in the basics of homemade dog food, the signs to watch out for, and when to consult the professionals. But what do you do when your vet or pet nutritionist recommends changes to your dog's diet based on health conditions or regular check-ups? Here, we'll explore how to adjust your recipes to keep up with your furry friend's evolving health needs.

Following Professional Recommendations

First and foremost, if your vet or pet nutritionist gives you specific guidelines or recommendations, those should be your primary roadmap. Whether it's adding a particular supplement, reducing fat content, or shifting to a different protein source, always adhere to these suggestions as closely as possible.

Gradual Transitions

Remember that sudden changes in diet can be hard on your dog's digestive system. Once you've gotten advice on what to modify, introduce these changes gradually. A good rule of thumb is to make adjustments over a period of 7-10 days, slowly mixing in the new food with the old to allow your dog's system to adapt.

Monitor and Adjust

Just as you keep an eye out for signs of nutritional imbalances, you'll want to watch for signs that the adjustments are having the desired effect. This might be something like increased energy, a shinier coat, or improved digestion. Alternatively, be alert for any negative symptoms like lethargy, skin issues, or gastrointestinal upset, and consult your vet if these arise.

Consider Specialized Recipes

Depending on your dog's specific health condition, your vet might recommend specialized recipes that you can prepare at home. These recipes are carefully formulated to meet particular health needs and can be a lifeline when commercial options aren't suitable or available. Make sure to follow these recipes precisely to provide the therapeutic benefits your dog needs.

Keep Records

As you adjust your dog's diet, it's helpful to keep records. Jot down any changes you make, along with observations about how your dog is responding. This can be particularly useful information to bring along to vet appointments for an informed discussion about your dog's ongoing dietary needs.

Regular Check-Ins

After making changes to your dog's diet, schedule follow-up appointments with your vet to monitor how well the adjustments are working. This will likely include some of the same tests and examinations conducted during the initial check-up and will help you fine-tune your homemade recipes further.

Adjusting your dog's diet based on their health needs isn't a one-time task but an ongoing process. Your vigilance and willingness to adapt are crucial to ensuring your pet's long-term well-being. With the proper adjustments and regular monitoring, your homemade dog food can continue to be a cornerstone of your dog's happy, healthy life.

Share the Love for Our Furry Friends

Do you enjoy sharing things that make you happy? Well, here's a chance to spread that joy to other dog lovers! Our book, 'Homemade Healthy Dog Food Cookbook', is filled with recipes for delicious and nutritious dog food, and you can help others discover it.

By leaving a review, you're not just sharing your thoughts; you're guiding others to make their dogs' lives better. Your review can help...

- Dogs enjoy healthier meals.
- Families take better care of their pets.
- Others find joy in preparing homemade dog food.

Leaving a review is easy and free but can make a world of difference. Simply scan the QR code below to get started:

SCAN BELOW TO LEAVE A REVIEW

Thank you for joining our community of dog lovers and for making a positive impact. Every review brings more tails wagging with happiness!

Part Two - Delicious Recipes

Life Stage Recipes

Puppy Recipes

Puppies have specific nutritional requirements, and it's essential that they get the right balance of nutrients to support their rapid growth and development. Always introduce new foods to a puppy's diet gradually to avoid upsetting their stomach. If a puppy shows any signs of allergies or digestive upset, consult a veterinarian. Remember, the recipes provided are not a comprehensive diet, so it's essential to ensure that puppies receive a balanced intake over time or supplement with essential nutrients when needed.

Chicken and Vegetable Puppy Stew

Ingredients:
- 1 pound boneless chicken thighs or breasts, cut into small pieces
- 1 cup brown rice
- 2 cups water or unsalted chicken broth
- 1 carrot, diced
- 1/2 cup peas (frozen or fresh)
- 1/2 cup green beans, chopped
- 1 tablespoon olive oil

Directions:
1. In a large pot, heat the olive oil over medium heat. Add the chicken pieces and cook until they are browned.
2. Add the brown rice, water or broth, carrot, peas, and green beans.
3. Bring the mixture to a boil, then reduce heat and let it simmer for about 20 minutes, or until the rice is cooked and vegetables are tender.
4. Allow to cool before serving. Store leftovers in the fridge.

Beef and Quinoa Power Bowl

Ingredients:
- 1 pound lean ground beef
- 1 cup quinoa
- 2 cups water
- 1/2 cup finely chopped spinach
- 1/4 cup grated zucchini
- 1/4 cup pumpkin puree

Directions:

1. In a pan, cook the ground beef until fully browned.
2. In a separate pot, bring 2 cups of water to boil and add quinoa. Let it simmer until fully cooked.
3. Once the beef and quinoa are cooked, mix them in a large bowl and add the spinach, zucchini, and pumpkin puree.
4. Stir everything well, let it cool, and then serve. Store any leftovers in the refrigerator.

Fish and Sweet Potato Mash

Ingredients:
- 1 pound of boneless salmon or white fish fillets
- 1 medium sweet potato, boiled and mashed
- 1 tablespoon flaxseed oil or fish oil
- 1/4 cup peas
- 1/4 cup finely chopped broccoli

Directions:
1. Steam or grill the fish until it's fully cooked.
2. In a bowl, mix the mashed sweet potato, flaxseed or fish oil, peas, and broccoli.
3. Flake the cooked fish into the bowl and mix well.
4. Allow to cool before serving. Store any leftovers in the fridge.

Turkey and Oats Delight

Ingredients:
- 1 pound ground turkey
- 1 cup rolled oats
- 2 1/2 cups water
- 1/2 apple, finely chopped (ensure no seeds)
- 1/4 cup plain yogurt (ensure no added sweeteners or flavors)

Directions:
1. In a pan, cook the ground turkey until browned.
2. In a separate pot, boil the oats in water until they become soft.
3. Combine the cooked turkey and oats in a bowl. Add in the chopped apple and stir.
4. Once cooled, top each serving with a dollop of plain yogurt.
5. Store any leftovers in the fridge.

Adult Dog Recipes

As with the puppy recipes, always introduce new foods slowly and monitor for any adverse reactions. Consult with a veterinarian regarding your dog's specific dietary needs and remember that these recipes should be part of a balanced diet, especially if feeding these recipes regularly.

Chicken and Lentil Bowl

Ingredients:
- 1 pound boneless chicken thighs or breasts, cut into bite-sized pieces
- 1 cup green lentils, rinsed and drained
- 3 cups water or unsalted chicken broth
- 1 carrot, diced
- 1/2 cup green beans, chopped
- 1/4 cup peas
- 1 tablespoon coconut oil or olive oil

Directions:
1. In a pot, heat the oil over medium heat. Add the chicken and brown lightly.
2. Add the lentils, water or broth, carrots, green beans, and peas.
3. Bring to a boil, then reduce heat and simmer for 25-30 minutes or until the lentils are tender.
4. Allow to cool before serving. Store leftovers in the fridge.

Beef and Barley Soup

Ingredients:
- 1 pound lean beef chunks (suitable for stewing)
- 3 cups water or unsalted beef broth
- 1/2 cup pearl barley
- 1 zucchini, chopped
- 1/4 cup celery, chopped
- 1/4 cup bell peppers, chopped (red or green)
- 1 tablespoon olive oil

Directions:
1. In a pot, heat the olive oil and brown the beef chunks.
2. Add the water or broth, followed by barley, zucchini, celery, and bell peppers.
3. Bring the mixture to a boil, reduce heat, and simmer for 40-45 minutes or until the barley is cooked and the beef is tender.
4. Cool down before serving. Refrigerate any leftovers.

Salmon and Brown Rice Dinner

Ingredients:
- 1 pound salmon fillet
- 1 cup brown rice
- 2 1/2 cups water or fish broth
- 1/2 cup chopped broccoli

- 1/2 cup chopped cauliflower
- 1 tablespoon fish oil or flaxseed oil

Directions:

1. In a pot, boil the brown rice in water or fish broth until cooked.
2. Steam or grill the salmon until fully cooked, then flake it into small pieces.
3. In a large bowl, combine the rice, salmon, broccoli, cauliflower, and fish or flaxseed oil.
4. Mix well, allow to cool, and serve. Keep leftovers in the fridge.

Turkey and Pumpkin Stew

Ingredients:

- 1 pound ground turkey
- 1 cup pumpkin puree
- 1/2 cup peas
- 1/4 cup cranberries (ensure no added sugars or spices)
- 1 apple, finely chopped (ensure no seeds)
- 1 tablespoon coconut oil
- 2 1/2 cups water

Directions:

1. In a pot, heat the coconut oil and brown the ground turkey.
2. Add the water, pumpkin puree, peas, cranberries, and apple.
3. Bring the mixture to a simmer, and cook for 20-25 minutes, stirring occasionally.
4. Once cooked, let it cool before serving. Refrigerate any leftovers.

Senior Dog Recipes

Senior dogs often have different dietary requirements than younger dogs, as they may be less active, have slower metabolisms, or have age-related health conditions. These recipes are tailored with that in mind, focusing on easy digestibility, lower fat content, and nutrient richness. Senior dogs can have delicate digestive systems or underlying health issues. Always introduce new foods gradually and monitor for any reactions. These recipes should complement a balanced diet tailored to your senior dog's needs. Always consult with a veterinarian before making significant changes to a dog's diet, especially for senior dogs.

Gentle Chicken and Rice

Ingredients:
- 1 pound boneless, skinless chicken thighs or breasts
- 1 1/2 cups white rice
- 3 1/2 cups water or unsalted chicken broth
- 1/2 cup carrots, finely chopped
- 1/4 cup green beans, finely chopped
- 1 tablespoon olive oil

Directions:
1. Heat the olive oil in a pot and lightly brown the chicken.
2. Add the water or broth and rice. Bring to a boil.
3. Reduce heat and add carrots and green beans.
4. Simmer until the rice is fully cooked and the chicken is tender, typically 20-25 minutes.
5. Allow to cool before serving. Refrigerate any leftovers.

Low-Fat Fish and Veggie Mix

Ingredients:
- 1 pound white fish (e.g., cod, haddock)
- 1 cup quinoa
- 2 1/2 cups water or fish stock
- 1/2 cup spinach, finely chopped
- 1/4 cup pumpkin puree
- 1 tablespoon flaxseed oil

Directions:
1. Steam or boil the fish until fully cooked. Once cooled, flake into small pieces.
2. In a separate pot, cook the quinoa in water or fish stock.
3. Once quinoa is cooked, mix with the flaked fish, spinach, pumpkin puree, and flaxseed oil.
4. Let it cool and then serve. Store leftovers in the fridge.

Soft Turkey and Sweet Potato Mash

Ingredients:
- 1 pound ground turkey
- 1 large sweet potato, boiled and mashed

- 1/2 cup peas
- 1/4 cup cooked oatmeal
- 1 tablespoon olive or coconut oil

Directions:

1. In a pan, cook the ground turkey with the oil until fully browned.
2. Mix the cooked turkey with the mashed sweet potato, peas, and oatmeal.
3. Stir until well combined. Let it cool and serve. Refrigerate any leftovers.

Liver Boost Casserole

(Liver is nutrient-rich and can be good for senior dogs in moderation. However, too much can lead to vitamin A toxicity, so feed occasionally and consult a vet.)

Ingredients:

- 1/2 pound beef or chicken liver, finely chopped
- 1 cup brown rice
- 2 1/2 cups water or unsalted broth
- 1/4 cup carrots, finely chopped
- 1/4 cup zucchini, finely chopped
- 1 tablespoon olive oil

Directions:

1. Heat the olive oil in a pot and lightly sauté the liver until it's partially cooked.
2. Add the water or broth, rice, carrots, and zucchini.
3. Bring to a boil, reduce heat, and simmer until the rice is cooked and the liver is tender.
4. Cool down before serving. Store leftovers in the fridge.

Special Dietary Needs

Grain-Free Recipes

Grain-free recipes can be a great option for dogs with specific dietary sensitivities or allergies. Always introduce new foods to your dog's diet gradually to avoid digestive upsets. Monitor your dog for any allergic reactions or sensitivities when introducing new recipes and adjust as necessary. These grain-free recipes should be part of a balanced diet, and it's essential to ensure that your dog is receiving all required nutrients, especially if they're on a grain-free diet long term. Consult with a veterinarian for guidance.

Chicken and Veggie Medley

Ingredients:
- 1 pound boneless, skinless chicken thighs or breasts, cut into bite-sized pieces
- 2 cups water or unsalted chicken broth
- 1 cup sweet potato, cubed
- 1/2 cup green beans, chopped
- 1/2 cup broccoli florets
- 1 tablespoon coconut oil

Directions:
1. In a pot, heat the coconut oil and brown the chicken pieces.
2. Add water or broth, sweet potato cubes, green beans, and broccoli.
3. Bring to a boil, then reduce heat and simmer for about 20-25 minutes, until the chicken is cooked through, and the vegetables are tender.
4. Allow to cool before serving. Refrigerate leftovers.

Beef and Pumpkin Stew

Ingredients:
- 1 pound lean beef chunks (suitable for stewing)
- 2 cups water or unsalted beef broth
- 1 cup pumpkin puree
- 1/2 cup peas
- 1/2 cup carrots, finely chopped
- 1 tablespoon olive oil

Directions:
1. In a pot, heat the olive oil and brown the beef chunks.
2. Add the water or broth, followed by pumpkin puree, peas, and chopped carrots.

3. Bring to a simmer and cook for 30-40 minutes until beef is tender.
4. Cool down before serving. Refrigerate any leftovers.

Fish Delight with Mixed Veggies

Ingredients:
- 1 pound white fish fillets (e.g., cod, haddock)
- 2 cups water or fish broth
- 1 cup zucchini, chopped
- 1/2 cup bell peppers, finely chopped (any color)
- 1/2 cup spinach, finely chopped
- 1 tablespoon fish oil

Directions:
1. In a pot, boil or steam the fish until fully cooked. Flake into small pieces.
2. In the same pot, add water or fish broth, zucchini, bell peppers, and spinach.
3. Simmer for about 10-15 minutes, until vegetables are tender.
4. Mix in the flaked fish and fish oil. Let it cool before serving. Store leftovers in the fridge.

Turkey and Green Bean Casserole

Ingredients:
- 1 pound ground turkey
- 1 cup green beans, chopped
- 1/2 cup cauliflower florets
- 1/4 cup cranberries (ensure no added sugars or spices)
- 2 cups water or unsalted turkey broth
- 1 tablespoon coconut oil

Directions:
1. In a pot, heat the coconut oil and brown the ground turkey.
2. Add the water or broth, green beans, cauliflower, and cranberries.
3. Bring the mixture to a simmer, cooking for 20-25 minutes.
4. Once cooked, let it cool before serving. Refrigerate any leftovers.

Low-Fat Recipes

Low-fat diets can be beneficial for dogs that need to lose weight, have certain medical conditions, or require dietary fat restrictions for other reasons. When preparing low-fat recipes, ensure your dog is still receiving adequate nutrition. Essential fatty acids, like those from fish oil, are vital for overall health. Always introduce new foods slowly and monitor your dog for any adverse reactions. It's essential to consult with a veterinarian regarding your dog's specific dietary needs, especially if focusing on a low-fat diet for the long term.

Chicken and Vegetable Soup

Ingredients:
- 1 pound skinless, boneless chicken breasts
- 3 cups water or unsalted chicken broth
- 1 cup carrots, chopped
- 1/2 cup green beans, chopped
- 1/2 cup celery, chopped
- 1 cup cooked brown rice
- 1 tablespoon olive oil (optional)

Directions:
1. In a pot, simmer the chicken breasts in water or broth until fully cooked.
2. Remove the chicken, shred it, and return it to the pot.
3. Add the carrots, green beans, and celery.
4. Simmer until the vegetables are tender (about 15-20 minutes).
5. Stir in the cooked brown rice.
6. Allow to cool before serving. Refrigerate leftovers.

Fish and Zucchini Dinner

Ingredients:
- 1 pound white fish fillets (e.g., cod, tilapia)
- 2 cups water or fish broth
- 1 cup zucchini, diced
- 1/2 cup peas
- 1/2 cup cooked quinoa
- 1 tablespoon fish oil

Directions:
1. In a pot, steam or boil the fish fillets until fully cooked, then flake them into small pieces.
2. In the same pot, add the water or fish broth, zucchini, and peas.
3. Simmer for about 10-15 minutes until vegetables are tender.
4. Mix in the flaked fish, quinoa, and fish oil.
5. Cool before serving. Store leftovers in the fridge.

Turkey and Pumpkin Mash

Ingredients:
- 1 pound lean ground turkey

- 1 cup pumpkin puree
- 1/2 cup green beans, chopped
- 1/2 cup carrots, finely chopped
- 2 cups water or unsalted turkey broth
- 1 tablespoon olive oil (optional)

Directions:

1. In a pot, cook the ground turkey in the olive oil (if using) until fully browned.
2. Add the water or broth, pumpkin puree, green beans, and carrots.
3. Bring the mixture to a simmer and cook for about 20-25 minutes.
4. Let it cool before serving. Refrigerate leftovers.

Tofu and Vegetable Mix

Ingredients:

- 1 cup firm tofu, crumbled
- 1 cup broccoli, finely chopped
- 1/2 cup carrots, finely chopped
- 1/2 cup bell peppers, finely chopped
- 2 cups water or vegetable broth
- 1 tablespoon flaxseed oil

Directions:

1. In a pot, heat the water or vegetable broth.
2. Add the crumbled tofu, broccoli, carrots, and bell peppers.
3. Simmer until the vegetables are tender, about 15-20 minutes.
4. Mix in flaxseed oil after cooking.
5. Cool before serving. Store leftovers in the fridge.

Low-Calorie Recipes

Low-calorie diets can be beneficial for dogs that need to manage or reduce their weight. It's crucial to provide a balanced diet that's filling but not overly caloric. When preparing low-calorie recipes, it's important to ensure that your dog feels satiated after meals. Fiber-rich vegetables and lean proteins can help in this aspect. Always introduce new foods slowly to your dog's diet to monitor for any adverse reactions. As always, when making significant changes to a dog's diet or for specific health concerns, consult with a veterinarian.

Lean Chicken and Green Veggie Mix

Ingredients:
- 1 pound skinless, boneless chicken breasts
- 3 cups water or unsalted chicken broth
- 1 cup broccoli florets, chopped
- 1/2 cup green beans, chopped
- 1/2 cup spinach, finely chopped
- 1 cup cooked brown rice

Directions:
1. Boil the chicken breasts in water or broth until fully cooked.
2. Once cooked, shred the chicken and return it to the pot.
3. Add the broccoli, green beans, and spinach.
4. Simmer for 10-15 minutes until the vegetables are tender.
5. Stir in the brown rice.
6. Cool before serving. Refrigerate leftovers.

Vegetable and Fish Broth

Ingredients:
- 1 pound white fish fillets (e.g., cod, tilapia)
- 2 1/2 cups water or fish broth
- 1/2 cup celery, chopped
- 1/2 cup zucchini, diced
- 1/2 cup carrots, diced
- 1 tablespoon fish oil

Directions:
1. In a pot, boil the fish fillets until fully cooked and then flake them into small pieces.
2. In the same pot, add the celery, zucchini, and carrots to the water or broth.
3. Simmer for about 10-15 minutes, or until the vegetables are tender.
4. Add the flaked fish and fish oil.
5. Cool before serving. Store leftovers in the fridge.

Turkey and Cabbage Bowl

Ingredients:
- 1 pound lean ground turkey
- 2 cups cabbage, shredded

- 1/2 cup green beans, chopped
- 1 cup cooked quinoa
- 2 1/2 cups water or unsalted turkey broth
- 1 tablespoon olive oil (optional)

Directions:

1. In a pot, lightly cook the ground turkey with olive oil (if using) until fully browned.
2. Add the water or broth, shredded cabbage, and green beans.
3. Simmer for about 15-20 minutes.
4. Mix in the cooked quinoa.
5. Let it cool before serving. Refrigerate leftovers.

Green Bean and Carrot Medley

Ingredients:

- 1 cup green beans, chopped
- 1 cup carrots, chopped
- 1/2 cup bell peppers, finely chopped
- 1/2 cup lean cooked beef or chicken, shredded
- 2 1/2 cups water or unsalted broth (chicken or beef, depending on the protein used)
- 1 tablespoon flaxseed oil

Directions:

1. In a pot, bring the water or broth to a simmer.
2. Add the green beans, carrots, and bell peppers.
3. Simmer for 15-20 minutes, or until vegetables are tender.
4. Add the shredded meat and flaxseed oil.
5. Mix well and let it cool before serving. Refrigerate any leftovers.

High-Protein Recipes

High-protein diets can be excellent for very active dogs, working dogs, or dogs that need to gain some weight or muscle. High-protein diets can be excellent for specific purposes, but they may not be suitable for all dogs, especially if sustained over a long period. Always ensure that high-protein diets are balanced with other essential nutrients and consult with a veterinarian before making significant changes to a dog's diet.

Beefy Protein Platter

Ingredients:
- 1.5 pounds lean ground beef
- 1/2 cup liver (chicken or beef), finely chopped
- 1/2 cup kidney (beef or pork), finely chopped
- 1 cup quinoa (cooked)
- 1 tablespoon flaxseed oil
- 1 egg (optional for an extra protein boost)

Directions:
1. In a pot or pan, brown the ground beef.
2. Add the finely chopped liver and kidney. Cook thoroughly.
3. Stir in the cooked quinoa.
4. If using, crack the egg into the mix and stir until well-cooked.
5. Finish with flaxseed oil. Allow the mix to cool before serving. Store leftovers in the fridge.

Chicken Muscle Mix

Ingredients:
- 1.5 pounds boneless, skinless chicken breasts or thighs, diced
- 1 cup cottage cheese
- 1 cup lentils (cooked)
- 1 egg
- 1 tablespoon fish oil

Directions:
1. In a pot, boil or steam the chicken pieces until cooked through.
2. Mix in the cooked lentils and cottage cheese.
3. Crack the egg into the mix, stirring until the egg is fully cooked.
4. Stir in the fish oil. Let the mixture cool before serving. Refrigerate any leftovers.

Fish Protein Pot

Ingredients:
- 1.5 pounds salmon or mackerel fillets
- 1 cup peas
- 1 cup chickpeas (cooked)
- 1 tablespoon fish oil
- 1 egg (optional)

Directions:

1. In a pot, steam or boil the fish fillets until cooked through, then flake them into smaller pieces.
2. Add peas and cooked chickpeas to the mix.
3. If using, add the egg and stir until it's well-cooked.
4. Mix in the fish oil. Allow the mix to cool before serving. Store leftovers in the fridge.

Turkey and Egg Delight

Ingredients:
- 1.5 pounds ground turkey
- 1/2 cup turkey or chicken liver, finely chopped
- 1 cup kidney beans (cooked)
- 2 eggs
- 1 tablespoon olive oil

Directions:
1. In a pot or pan, cook the ground turkey thoroughly.
2. Add the chopped liver to the pot and ensure it's well-cooked.
3. Mix in the cooked kidney beans.
4. Crack the eggs into the mix, stirring until fully cooked.
5. Finish with olive oil. Allow the mix to cool before serving. Refrigerate leftovers.

Low-Sodium Recipes

For dogs with heart issues or certain other medical conditions, a low-sodium diet can be beneficial. Always ensure that you're using unsalted ingredients and broths when preparing these recipes. When preparing low-sodium recipes or any dietary change, it's crucial to ensure the dog receives all essential nutrients. Always introduce new foods slowly and monitor your dog for any adverse reactions. Especially when dealing with medical conditions, consulting with a veterinarian about specific dietary needs and changes is imperative.

Heart-Healthy Chicken and Veggies

Ingredients:
- 1 pound boneless, skinless chicken breasts
- 3 cups water
- 1 cup sweet potatoes, diced
- 1/2 cup green beans, chopped
- 1/2 cup carrots, chopped
- 1 cup brown rice (cooked)

Directions:
1. Place the chicken breasts and water in a pot and simmer until the chicken is fully cooked.
2. Remove the chicken, shred it, and set it aside.
3. In the same pot, add the sweet potatoes, green beans, and carrots.
4. Simmer until the vegetables are tender.
5. Mix in the shredded chicken and cooked rice.
6. Cool before serving. Refrigerate leftovers.

Low-Sodium Beef and Pumpkin Stew

Ingredients:
- 1 pound lean ground beef
- 3 cups water
- 1 cup pumpkin puree
- 1/2 cup peas
- 1 cup cooked quinoa

Directions:
1. In a pot, brown the ground beef thoroughly.
2. Add water, pumpkin puree, and peas.
3. Simmer for about 20 minutes.
4. Stir in the cooked quinoa.
5. Let the mixture cool before serving. Store leftovers in the refrigerator.

Fish and Vegetable Medley

Ingredients:
- 1 pound white fish fillets (e.g., cod, tilapia)
- 2 1/2 cups water

- 1 cup zucchini, diced
- 1/2 cup bell peppers, finely chopped
- 1/2 cup broccoli florets
- 1 tablespoon fish oil

Directions:

1. In a pot, steam or boil the fish fillets until fully cooked. Flake them into small pieces.
2. In the same pot, add the zucchini, bell peppers, and broccoli to the water.
3. Simmer for about 10-15 minutes, or until the vegetables are tender.
4. Add the flaked fish and fish oil.
5. Mix well and let it cool before serving. Store leftovers in the refrigerator.

Turkey and Green Bean Blend

Ingredients:

- 1 pound lean ground turkey
- 2 1/2 cups water
- 1 cup green beans, chopped
- 1/2 cup celery, chopped
- 1 cup cooked barley

Directions:

1. In a pot, cook the ground turkey until it's fully browned.
2. Add the water, green beans, and celery.
3. Bring the mixture to a simmer and cook for about 20-25 minutes.
4. Stir in the cooked barley.
5. Let it cool before serving. Store leftovers in the fridge.

Type of Protein Base

Chicken-Based Recipes

Chicken is a popular protein source for many dogs due to its lean profile and easy digestibility. Always make sure to introduce new recipes gradually to your dog's diet and observe for any potential allergies or intolerances. It's important to remove any bones from chicken before cooking, as cooked bones can be hazardous for dogs. If unsure about any ingredient or dietary changes, always consult with a veterinarian.

Classic Chicken and Rice

Ingredients:
- 1.5 pounds boneless, skinless chicken breasts or thighs
- 4 cups water
- 1 cup brown rice
- 1 cup carrots, diced
- 1/2 cup peas

Directions:
1. Place the chicken, water, and rice in a large pot.
2. Bring to a boil and then reduce to a simmer.
3. Once the chicken is almost fully cooked, add the carrots and peas.
4. Continue to simmer until the chicken is thoroughly cooked, and the vegetables are tender.
5. Allow to cool, then shred the chicken and mix well before serving. Store leftovers in the refrigerator.

Chicken and Veggie Stew

Ingredients:
- 1 pound boneless, skinless chicken breasts or thighs, diced
- 3 cups unsalted chicken broth
- 1 sweet potato, diced
- 1/2 cup green beans, chopped
- 1/2 cup broccoli florets

Directions:
1. In a pot, combine chicken pieces and broth. Bring to a simmer.
2. Once the chicken is half cooked, add sweet potato, green beans, and broccoli.
3. Continue cooking until the chicken is thoroughly cooked and the vegetables are tender.

4. Cool the stew before serving. Refrigerate leftovers.

Chicken Pasta Delight

Ingredients:
- 1.5 pounds boneless, skinless chicken breasts
- 3 cups water
- 1 cup pasta (choose a shape like rotini or penne)
- 1 zucchini, diced
- 1 tablespoon olive oil

Directions:
1. Boil the chicken breasts in water until fully cooked.
2. Remove the chicken and set aside. In the same water, cook the pasta until al dente.
3. As the pasta cooks, shred the chicken into bite-sized pieces.
4. Once the pasta is cooked, add the chicken, zucchini, and olive oil. Cook for another 5-7 minutes until the zucchini is soft.
5. Allow the mixture to cool before serving. Store any leftovers in the refrigerator.

Chicken and Berry Salad

Ingredients:
- 1 pound boneless, skinless chicken breasts, cooked and shredded
- 1/2 cup blueberries
- 1/2 cup cranberries (unsweetened)
- 1/2 cup cooked quinoa
- 1 tablespoon flaxseed oil

Directions:
1. In a mixing bowl, combine the shredded chicken, blueberries, cranberries, and quinoa.
2. Drizzle with flaxseed oil and mix well.
3. Serve at room temperature or slightly chilled. Refrigerate leftovers.

Beef-Based Recipes

Beef is a rich source of protein and can be a favorite for many dogs. Always ensure that the beef used in these recipes is lean, as excessive fat can be hard for some dogs to digest. Introduce any new recipes gradually into your dog's diet to check for any potential allergies or intolerances. When in doubt about any ingredients or dietary changes, consult with a veterinarian.

Beef and Barley Bowl

Ingredients:
- 1.5 pounds lean ground beef
- 3 cups water or unsalted beef broth
- 1 cup barley
- 1 cup carrots, diced
- 1/2 cup peas

Directions:
1. In a pot, brown the ground beef.
2. Add water or unsalted beef broth and barley to the pot and bring to a boil.
3. Once boiling, reduce to a simmer and add carrots and peas.
4. Cook until the barley is tender and the beef is fully cooked.
5. Allow the mixture to cool before serving. Store leftovers in the refrigerator.

Beef and Veggie Stew

Ingredients:
- 1 pound beef stew meat, diced
- 2 1/2 cups unsalted beef broth
- 1 sweet potato, diced
- 1/2 cup green beans, chopped
- 1/2 cup broccoli florets

Directions:
1. Place the beef stew meat and broth in a pot and bring to a simmer.
2. Once the beef starts to soften, add the sweet potato, green beans, and broccoli.
3. Continue to simmer until the beef is tender and the vegetables are cooked through.
4. Cool before serving and refrigerate any leftovers.

Beef Pasta Mix

Ingredients:
- 1.5 pounds lean ground beef
- 3 cups water
- 1 cup pasta (choose shapes like fusilli or shells)
- 1 zucchini, diced
- 1 tablespoon olive oil

Directions:
1. In a pot, cook the ground beef until it's browned.
2. Remove the beef and set aside. In the same water, cook the pasta until al dente.

3. Once the pasta is almost done, add the cooked beef, diced zucchini, and olive oil.
4. Continue cooking for about 5-7 minutes until the zucchini is soft.
5. Allow to cool before serving. Store leftovers in the fridge.

Beef and Pumpkin Puree

Ingredients:
- 1 pound lean ground beef
- 1 cup pumpkin puree
- 1/2 cup cooked quinoa
- 1 tablespoon flaxseed oil
- A pinch of turmeric (optional)

Directions:
1. In a pan, cook the ground beef until fully browned.
2. Once cooked, mix in the pumpkin puree and cooked quinoa.
3. Drizzle the flaxseed oil over the mixture.
4. If you choose to, sprinkle a pinch of turmeric for added health benefits (anti-inflammatory properties).
5. Mix well, cool before serving, and store any leftovers in the refrigerator.

Fish-Based Recipes

Fish is a fantastic source of omega-3 fatty acids, which can be beneficial for a dog's skin, coat, and overall health. It's important to ensure that the fish used in these recipes is free from bones. Always introduce new foods slowly and monitor your dog for any adverse reactions. When in doubt about any ingredient or dietary changes, always consult with a veterinarian.

Simple Salmon Delight

Ingredients:
- 1 pound salmon fillet (skinless and boneless)
- 2 1/2 cups water or unsalted fish broth
- 1 cup sweet potato, diced
- 1/2 cup green peas
- 1 tablespoon olive oil

Directions:
1. In a pot, add the salmon and water or fish broth.
2. Bring to a boil and then simmer until the salmon is cooked through.
3. Add the sweet potato and peas and continue cooking until the vegetables are tender.
4. Once cooked, flake the salmon into smaller pieces and mix well.
5. Drizzle with olive oil, let it cool, then serve. Store leftovers in the fridge.

White Fish and Quinoa Bowl

Ingredients:
- 1 pound white fish (e.g., cod, tilapia), boneless
- 3 cups water
- 1 cup quinoa
- 1 cup zucchini, diced
- 1/2 cup carrots, chopped

Directions:
1. Place fish and water in a pot and simmer until the fish is cooked.
2. Remove the fish and flake it into smaller pieces. Set aside.
3. In the same water, add the quinoa and cook as directed.
4. Add the zucchini and carrots during the last 10 minutes of the quinoa cooking.
5. Mix the flaked fish back into the pot, let it cool, then serve. Refrigerate any leftovers.

Tuna and Rice Mix

Ingredients:
- 2 cans of tuna in water, drained
- 2 cups cooked brown rice
- 1/2 cup broccoli florets, steamed and chopped
- 1/2 cup spinach, steamed and chopped
- 1 tablespoon fish oil

Directions:
1. In a large bowl, mix the drained tuna and cooked rice.

2. Add the steamed broccoli and spinach, mixing thoroughly.
3. Drizzle with fish oil to boost the omega-3 content.
4. Allow the mixture to cool before serving. Store leftovers in the refrigerator.

Sardine and Veggie Mash

Ingredients:
- 2 cans of sardines in water, drained
- 1 cup mashed pumpkin or butternut squash
- 1/2 cup cooked green beans, chopped
- 1/2 cup cooked carrots, chopped
- 1 tablespoon flaxseed oil (optional)

Directions:
1. In a large bowl, mash the sardines.
2. Add the mashed pumpkin or butternut squash, green beans, and carrots.
3. Mix until well combined.
4. Optionally, you can drizzle with flaxseed oil for added omega-3s.
5. Let it cool before serving. Refrigerate leftovers.

Lamb-Based Recipes

Lamb is a protein-rich option that's often well-tolerated by dogs, even some with food sensitivities. As with any dietary changes or introduction of new foods, monitor your dog for any adverse reactions. Make sure to remove any bones or fat from the lamb meat. It's always best to consult with a veterinarian when unsure about ingredients or dietary changes.

Lamb and Lentil Stew

Ingredients:
- 1.5 pounds lamb stew meat, cubed
- 3 cups water or unsalted broth
- 1 cup green lentils
- 1 cup carrots, diced
- 1/2 cup peas

Directions:
1. In a pot, combine lamb cubes and water/broth. Bring to a simmer.
2. Once the lamb starts to soften, add lentils and carrots.
3. Continue to simmer until the lamb is tender and the lentils are fully cooked.
4. Add peas in the last 10 minutes of cooking.
5. Allow to cool before serving. Store leftovers in the refrigerator.

Ground Lamb and Veggie Mix

Ingredients:
- 1.5 pounds ground lamb
- 2 1/2 cups unsalted beef or vegetable broth
- 1 cup sweet potatoes, diced
- 1/2 cup green beans, chopped
- 1 tablespoon olive oil

Directions:
1. Brown the ground lamb in a pot.
2. Add the broth and bring to a boil.
3. Add the sweet potatoes and green beans and simmer until fully cooked.
4. Drizzle with olive oil, mix well, and allow to cool before serving. Refrigerate leftovers.

Lamb and Rice Delight

Ingredients:
- 1.5 pounds boneless lamb meat, chopped
- 3 cups water
- 1 cup brown rice
- 1/2 cup broccoli florets
- 1/2 cup zucchini, diced

Directions:
1. In a pot, combine the lamb meat and water. Bring to a simmer.
2. As the lamb cooks, add brown rice.

3. Once the rice is half-cooked, add broccoli and zucchini.
4. Continue simmering until the lamb is fully cooked, and the rice is tender.
5. Let the mixture cool before serving. Store any leftovers in the fridge.

Lamb Pasta Feast

Ingredients:
- 1 pound ground lamb
- 2 1/2 cups water
- 1 cup pasta (choose shapes like fusilli or rigatoni)
- 1/2 cup spinach, steamed and chopped
- 1 tablespoon flaxseed oil

Directions:
1. In a pot, brown the ground lamb.
2. Add water and bring to a boil.
3. Add pasta and cook until al dente.
4. Mix in the steamed spinach during the last couple of minutes.
5. Drizzle the flaxseed oil over the top for added health benefits.
6. Once cooled down, it's ready to serve. Refrigerate any remaining portions.

Vegetarian/Vegan Recipes

Here are some vegetarian/vegan recipes for dogs. Remember, while dogs have evolved as omnivores and can digest plant-based foods, a completely vegetarian or vegan diet may not provide them with all the essential nutrients they need. If you're considering such a diet for your dog, always work closely with a veterinarian to ensure your pet's nutritional needs are fully met. Always consult with a veterinarian before making major changes to your pet's diet. Supplements like taurine, L-carnitine, and certain B vitamins might be necessary to ensure the dog's health.

Vegetarian Quinoa and Veggie Bowl

Ingredients:
- 2 cups cooked quinoa
- 1 cup sweet potatoes, diced
- 1/2 cup carrots, diced
- 1/2 cup green beans, chopped
- 1/4 cup peas
- 1 tablespoon olive or flaxseed oil
- Taurine supplement (as recommended by a vet)

Directions:
1. Steam or boil the sweet potatoes, carrots, green beans, and peas until tender.
2. Mix the cooked vegetables with quinoa.
3. Drizzle with olive or flaxseed oil and mix well.
4. Add taurine supplement as per vet's recommendation.
5. Once cooled, serve to your pup and store leftovers in the refrigerator.

Vegan Lentil and Veggie Stew

Ingredients:
- 1 cup green or brown lentils
- 2 1/2 cups water
- 1 cup butternut squash, diced
- 1/2 cup broccoli florets
- 1/2 cup spinach, chopped
- 1 tablespoon nutritional yeast (for B vitamins)
- Taurine supplement (as recommended by a vet)

Directions:
1. In a pot, combine lentils and water. Bring to a boil, then reduce to a simmer.
2. Add butternut squash and broccoli and continue to simmer until lentils are cooked and veggies are tender.
3. Stir in the spinach just until wilted.
4. Mix in nutritional yeast and taurine supplement.
5. Let the mixture cool before serving. Refrigerate any leftovers.

Vegetarian Chickpea and Rice Medley

Ingredients:

- 1 cup chickpeas (canned or soaked and boiled)
- 1 cup cooked brown rice
- 1/2 cup zucchini, diced
- 1/2 cup bell peppers, diced
- 1 tablespoon olive oil
- Taurine supplement (as recommended by a vet)

Directions:

1. If using dried chickpeas, soak overnight and then boil until tender.
2. Mix chickpeas and brown rice in a bowl.
3. Steam or sauté zucchini and bell peppers just until soft, then mix into the bowl.
4. Drizzle with olive oil.
5. Add taurine supplement as per vet's advice.
6. Let it cool down before serving. Store the remaining portions in the fridge.

Vegan Vegetable and Tofu Scramble

Ingredients:

- 1 cup tofu, crumbled
- 1/2 cup green peas
- 1/2 cup carrots, grated
- 1/4 cup nutritional yeast
- 1 tablespoon coconut oil
- Turmeric (just a pinch for color and anti-inflammatory properties)
- Taurine supplement (as recommended by a vet)

Directions:

1. Heat coconut oil in a pan and sauté crumbled tofu until slightly golden.
2. Add green peas and grated carrots. Continue to sauté until vegetables are tender.
3. Sprinkle in the nutritional yeast and a pinch of turmeric, mixing well.
4. Add taurine supplement as per vet's recommendation.
5. Allow the scramble to cool before serving. Keep leftovers refrigerated.

Meal Types

Breakfast Dishes Recipes

Breakfast dishes can provide a delightful start to your dog's day. Always remember to introduce any new foods slowly and watch for any signs of allergies or digestive issues. If you're unsure about any ingredient or the appropriate serving size for your dog's weight and activity level, it's best to consult with a veterinarian.

Sunny Egg and Spinach Scramble

Ingredients:
- 2 eggs
- 1/2 cup fresh spinach, chopped
- 1 tablespoon coconut or olive oil
- A pinch of turmeric (optional, for anti-inflammatory properties)

Directions:
1. Heat oil in a pan over medium heat.
2. Whisk the eggs in a bowl and pour them into the pan.
3. Add the chopped spinach and turmeric.
4. Scramble until the eggs are fully cooked.
5. Let it cool before serving.

Morning Oats and Berry Delight

Ingredients:
- 1 cup cooked oatmeal (ensure it's cooled)
- 1/4 cup blueberries
- 1/4 cup chopped strawberries
- 1 tablespoon flaxseed or chia seeds (ground)
- A drizzle of honey (optional)

Directions:
1. Prepare oatmeal according to package instructions and let it cool.
2. Mix in the blueberries and strawberries.
3. Sprinkle the ground flaxseed or chia seeds on top.
4. Optionally, drizzle a little honey for added sweetness.
5. Serve in your dog's dish.

Peanut Butter and Banana Pancakes

Ingredients:
- 1/2 cup whole wheat flour
- 1/4 cup rolled oats
- 1 ripe banana, mashed
- 1 egg
- 2 tablespoons natural peanut butter (ensure it doesn't contain xylitol)
- Enough water to make a batter

Directions:
1. In a bowl, mix the flour and oats.
2. Add the mashed banana, egg, and peanut butter. Mix well.
3. Gradually add water until a batter consistency is achieved.
4. Heat a non-stick pan over medium heat.
5. Drop spoonfuls of the batter onto the pan to form small pancakes.
6. Cook until bubbles form on top, then flip and cook the other side.
7. Allow the pancakes to cool before serving.

Chicken and Veggie Breakfast Hash

Ingredients:
- 1/2 cup cooked chicken breast, shredded
- 1/4 cup sweet potatoes, diced
- 1/4 cup green bell peppers, diced
- 1/4 cup zucchini, diced
- 1 tablespoon olive oil

Directions:
1. In a pan, heat the olive oil over medium heat.
2. Add the sweet potatoes and cook until they start to soften.
3. Add the bell peppers and zucchini, continuing to sauté until all veggies are tender.
4. Stir in the shredded chicken breast and cook until everything is heated through.
5. Remove from heat and allow to cool before serving.

Light Lunches/Snacks Recipes

Light lunches or snacks are great for midday treats or for times when you might want to give your dog a little something extra between meals. Always monitor your dog when introducing a new treat or snack to ensure there are no adverse reactions. And remember, treats should only constitute a small portion of your dog's overall caloric intake.

Veggie and Fruit Pupsicles

Ingredients:
- 1/2 cup carrot juice (unsweetened)
- 1/2 cup blueberries
- 1/2 cup diced apple (ensure no seeds)
- 1/2 cup water

Directions:
1. Mix carrot juice and water in a bowl.
2. Add blueberries and diced apple pieces to popsicle molds or ice cube trays.
3. Pour the carrot juice mixture over the fruit.
4. Freeze until solid, then serve as a refreshing treat!

Peanut Butter and Banana Bites

Ingredients:
- 1 ripe banana, mashed
- 2 tablespoons natural peanut butter (ensure it doesn't contain xylitol)
- 1 cup oat flour

Directions:
1. Preheat your oven to 350°F (175°C).
2. In a bowl, combine mashed banana and peanut butter.
3. Gradually mix in oat flour until you get a dough-like consistency.
4. Roll out the dough and cut into bite-sized pieces or shapes using cookie cutters.
5. Place on a parchment-lined baking sheet and bake for 12-15 minutes.
6. Cool before serving. Store in an airtight container.

Chicken Jerky Strips (Baked)

Ingredients:
- 2 boneless, skinless chicken breasts

Directions:
1. Preheat your oven to 200°F (90°C).
2. Clean and trim any excess fat from the chicken breasts.
3. Slice the chicken into thin strips, about 1/4 inch thick.
4. Place the strips on a parchment-lined baking sheet, ensuring they don't touch.
5. Bake for 2 hours or until the strips are dried and hard.
6. Allow to cool. Store in an airtight container.

Sweet Potato Chew Sticks

Ingredients:
- 2 medium sweet potatoes, washed

Directions:
1. Preheat your oven to 250°F (120°C).
2. Slice the sweet potatoes lengthwise into strips about 1/3 inch thick.
3. Place the strips on a baking sheet lined with parchment paper.
4. Bake for about 2.5 to 3 hours, turning halfway through, until they are dry and a bit chewy.
5. Allow to cool before serving. Store in an airtight container.

Dinner Recipes

As always, remember to introduce new foods gradually and observe for any adverse reactions. Additionally, consult with a veterinarian regarding any concerns about ingredients or portion sizes for your dog.

Beefy Veggie Medley

Ingredients:
- 1 pound lean ground beef
- 1 cup brown rice, cooked
- 1/2 cup carrots, diced
- 1/2 cup peas
- 1/4 cup pumpkin puree (not pie filling)
- 1 tablespoon olive oil

Directions:
1. In a large skillet, brown the ground beef over medium heat, breaking it apart as it cooks.
2. Add the carrots and peas, cooking until the vegetables are tender.
3. Stir in the cooked rice and pumpkin puree until well mixed.
4. Drizzle with olive oil and mix thoroughly.
5. Allow to cool before serving.

Chicken and Barley Stew

Ingredients:
- 1.5 pounds chicken thighs or breasts, diced
- 3 cups water or unsalted chicken broth
- 1 cup barley
- 1/2 cup green beans, chopped
- 1/2 cup celery, diced
- 1 tablespoon coconut oil

Directions:
1. In a pot, combine the diced chicken and water or broth. Bring to a boil.
2. Reduce heat to medium and add barley.
3. As the barley cooks, add green beans and celery.
4. Simmer until the chicken is fully cooked and the barley is tender.
5. Mix in the coconut oil for added gloss and health benefits.
6. Let it cool down before serving. Store leftovers in the refrigerator.

Fish and Sweet Potato Mash

Ingredients:
- 1 pound white fish fillets (like cod or tilapia)
- 2 medium sweet potatoes, peeled and cubed
- 1/2 cup peas
- 1 tablespoon olive oil
- A pinch of turmeric (optional)

Directions:

1. Steam or boil the sweet potatoes until they are soft.
2. In a separate pan, cook the fish fillets until they're fully cooked and flake easily.
3. Mash the sweet potatoes and mix in the peas and olive oil.
4. Flake the fish and gently mix it into the sweet potato mash.
5. Add a pinch of turmeric if desired.
6. Once cooled, it's ready to serve.

Lamb and Quinoa Mix

Ingredients:
- 1 pound lamb meat, diced
- 2 cups cooked quinoa
- 1/2 cup broccoli florets, steamed
- 1/2 cup zucchini, diced and steamed
- 1 tablespoon flaxseed oil

Directions:
1. In a skillet, cook the diced lamb until it's browned and fully cooked.
2. Mix the cooked lamb with the quinoa in a bowl.
3. Add the steamed broccoli and zucchini to the bowl.
4. Drizzle with flaxseed oil and mix everything well.
5. Allow the mixture to cool before serving to your dog.

Functional Foods

Immune-Boosting Recipes

Immune-boosting foods can be beneficial for dogs, especially when they contain antioxidants, vitamins, and minerals. Always introduce new foods gradually to avoid any digestive upset and observe for any adverse reactions. Additionally, these recipes are meant to complement a well-balanced diet and should not replace regular meals entirely. Consulting with a veterinarian regarding any concerns about ingredients or portion sizes for your dog is always recommended.

Turmeric and Chicken Stew

Ingredients:
- 1.5 pounds chicken thighs or breasts, diced
- 3 cups unsalted chicken broth
- 1 cup carrots, sliced
- 1/2 cup green beans, chopped
- 1 tablespoon turmeric powder
- 1 tablespoon coconut oil

Directions:
1. In a pot, bring the chicken broth to a boil.
2. Add the diced chicken and cook until halfway done.
3. Add the carrots and green beans.
4. Once the chicken is fully cooked and the veggies are tender, stir in the turmeric and coconut oil.
5. Let the stew cool before serving.

Berry and Spinach Blend

Ingredients:
- 1 cup blueberries
- 1 cup strawberries, chopped
- 2 cups fresh spinach, chopped
- 1 tablespoon chia seeds
- 1 cup plain, unsweetened yogurt

Directions:
1. In a blender, combine blueberries, strawberries, and spinach. Blend until smooth.
2. Pour the mixture into a bowl.

3. Stir in the chia seeds and yogurt.
4. Serve a portion appropriate for your dog's size and store the rest in the refrigerator.

Beef and Pumpkin Mix

Ingredients:
- 1 pound lean ground beef
- 1 cup pumpkin puree (not pie filling)
- 1/2 cup quinoa, cooked
- 1 tablespoon olive oil
- A pinch of dried rosemary

Directions:
1. In a skillet, cook the ground beef until fully browned.
2. In a mixing bowl, combine the beef, pumpkin puree, and cooked quinoa.
3. Drizzle with olive oil and sprinkle with dried rosemary.
4. Mix everything well and let it cool before serving.

Omega Fish Feast

Ingredients:
- 1 pound salmon fillets
- 1 cup sweet potatoes, steamed and mashed
- 1 tablespoon flaxseed oil
- 1/2 cup green peas

Directions:
1. Grill or steam the salmon fillets until fully cooked.
2. Flake the salmon into bite-sized pieces.
3. Mix the salmon, mashed sweet potatoes, and green peas in a bowl.
4. Drizzle with flaxseed oil for a dose of omega-3 fatty acids.
5. Allow the mixture to cool before serving.

Bone and Joint Health Recipes

Bone and joint health are crucial for dogs, especially as they age. Nutrients like omega-3 fatty acids, chondroitin, glucosamine, and certain antioxidants can benefit joint health. Always introduce new foods gradually to monitor for any adverse reactions. Consult with a veterinarian to ensure these meals align with your dog's specific health needs. Here are some recipes that focus on nutrients known to support joint health and bone density:

Salmon and Green - Lipped Mussel Medley

Ingredients:
- 1 pound salmon fillets
- 1/4 cup green-lipped mussel powder
- 1 cup quinoa, cooked
- 1 tablespoon fish oil
- 1/2 cup broccoli, steamed and chopped

Directions:
1. Grill or steam the salmon fillets until fully cooked.
2. Flake the salmon into bite-sized pieces.
3. In a bowl, mix the salmon, quinoa, and broccoli.
4. Sprinkle the green-lipped mussel powder and drizzle with fish oil. Mix well.
5. Allow to cool before serving.

Chicken and Bone Broth Soup

Ingredients:
- 1.5 pounds chicken thighs or breasts
- 4 cups homemade unsalted bone broth (or a high-quality store-bought version without additives)
- 1 cup carrots, diced
- 1/2 cup green beans, chopped
- 1 tablespoon turmeric powder

Directions:
1. In a pot, bring the bone broth to a boil.
2. Add the diced chicken, carrots, and green beans.
3. Simmer until the chicken is fully cooked and vegetables are tender.
4. Stir in the turmeric powder.
5. Let it cool before serving.

Beef and Chia Seeds Mix

Ingredients:
- 1 pound lean ground beef
- 1 cup brown rice, cooked
- 2 tablespoons chia seeds
- 1/2 cup pumpkin puree
- 1 tablespoon coconut oil

Directions:

1. In a skillet, brown the ground beef fully.
2. In a mixing bowl, combine the beef, rice, pumpkin puree, and chia seeds.
3. Drizzle with coconut oil and mix thoroughly.
4. Allow to cool before serving.

Egg and Sardine Feast

Ingredients:
- 2 whole sardines, cleaned and de-boned (or use canned sardines in water)
- 2 boiled eggs, chopped
- 1 cup spinach, steamed and chopped
- 1 tablespoon flaxseed oil

Directions:
1. If using fresh sardines, either grill or steam them until fully cooked.
2. In a bowl, break up the sardines and mix with the chopped boiled eggs.
3. Add the steamed spinach to the bowl.
4. Drizzle with flaxseed oil and mix everything together.
5. Allow to cool before serving.

Skin and Coat Health Recipes

A dog's skin and coat health can be influenced by the nutrients they consume. Omega-3 and Omega-6 fatty acids, in particular, play a crucial role in maintaining a shiny coat and healthy skin. The consistent inclusion of oils rich in essential fatty acids (like fish oil, flaxseed oil, and safflower oil) in your dog's diet can enhance the health of their skin and coat. Always introduce new foods gradually to observe for any adverse reactions, and always consult with a veterinarian regarding dietary changes or concerns.

Flaxseed and Salmon Delight

Ingredients:
- 1 pound salmon fillets
- 1 cup sweet potatoes, steamed and mashed
- 1 tablespoon ground flaxseed
- 1/2 cup peas
- 1 tablespoon olive oil

Directions:
1. Grill or steam the salmon fillets until fully cooked.
2. Flake the salmon into bite-sized pieces.
3. In a bowl, combine salmon, mashed sweet potatoes, and peas.
4. Stir in ground flaxseed and drizzle with olive oil.
5. Allow to cool before serving.

Egg and Oatmeal Breakfast

Ingredients:
- 2 eggs, scrambled or boiled
- 1 cup cooked oatmeal
- 1 tablespoon fish oil
- 1/4 cup blueberries
- 1/4 cup plain, unsweetened yogurt

Directions:
1. Prepare the eggs to your dog's preference (scrambled or boiled).
2. Mix the eggs with cooked oatmeal in a bowl.
3. Add blueberries and yogurt.
4. Drizzle with fish oil and mix well.
5. Serve once cooled to a suitable temperature.

Chicken and Quinoa Bowl

Ingredients:
- 1.5 pounds chicken thighs or breasts, diced
- 1 cup quinoa, cooked
- 1/2 cup green beans, steamed and chopped
- 1 tablespoon coconut oil
- 1 tablespoon hemp seeds

Directions:

1. Cook the diced chicken in a pan until fully cooked.
2. In a bowl, mix the chicken, quinoa, and green beans.
3. Drizzle with coconut oil and sprinkle with hemp seeds.
4. Mix well and allow to cool before serving.

Liver and Vegetable Mix

Ingredients:
- 1 pound beef or chicken liver, finely diced
- 1 cup brown rice, cooked
- 1/2 cup carrots, steamed and diced
- 1/2 cup broccoli, steamed and chopped
- 1 tablespoon safflower oil

Directions:
1. In a pan, cook the liver pieces until fully cooked.
2. Combine liver, rice, carrots, and broccoli in a bowl.
3. Drizzle with safflower oil and mix well.
4. Allow to cool before serving.

Digestive Health Recipes

Digestive health is crucial for nutrient absorption and overall well-being. Ingredients rich in fiber, probiotics, and easily digestible proteins can be beneficial. Ingredients like pumpkin, ginger, and probiotic yogurt are known to be beneficial for canine digestive health. However, it's always essential to introduce new foods gradually and monitor for any adverse reactions. Always consult with a veterinarian regarding dietary changes, especially if your dog has existing digestive issues. Here are some recipes designed to support a dog's digestive system:

Pumpkin and Chicken Rice Bowl

Ingredients:
- 1.5 pounds chicken thighs or breasts, diced
- 1 cup brown rice, cooked
- 1 cup pumpkin puree (ensure it's 100% pure pumpkin and not pie filling)
- 1 tablespoon coconut oil
- A pinch of ginger powder

Directions:
1. Cook the diced chicken in a pan until fully cooked.
2. In a bowl, mix the chicken with rice and pumpkin puree.
3. Stir in coconut oil and ginger powder.
4. Allow to cool before serving.

Probiotic Yogurt and Berry Blend

Ingredients:
- 1 cup plain, unsweetened probiotic yogurt
- 1/2 cup blueberries
- 1/2 cup strawberries, chopped
- 1 tablespoon chia seeds
- A drizzle of honey (optional)

Directions:
1. In a bowl, mix yogurt with blueberries and strawberries.
2. Stir in chia seeds and drizzle with a bit of honey if desired (ensure it's a safe amount for your dog's size).
3. Serve in appropriate portion sizes based on your dog's weight.

Beet and Turkey Mash

Ingredients:
- 1 pound ground turkey
- 1 cup beets, steamed and diced
- 1/2 cup quinoa, cooked
- 1 tablespoon flaxseed oil
- A sprinkle of dried rosemary

Directions:
1. Brown the ground turkey in a skillet.

2. In a bowl, combine turkey, beets, and quinoa.
3. Drizzle with flaxseed oil and sprinkle with dried rosemary.
4. Mix well and allow to cool before serving.

Sweet Potato and Fish Fillet

Ingredients:
- 1 pound white fish fillets (cod or tilapia)
- 1 cup sweet potatoes, steamed and mashed
- 1/2 cup green peas, steamed
- 1 tablespoon olive oil
- A pinch of turmeric powder

Directions:
1. Grill or steam the fish fillets until fully cooked.
2. Flake the fish into bite-sized pieces.
3. In a bowl, mix the fish, mashed sweet potatoes, and green peas.
4. Stir in olive oil and turmeric powder.
5. Allow to cool before serving.

Treats and Snacks

Biscuits and Crunchy Treat Recipes

Homemade biscuits and crunchy treats can be a delightful way to reward your dog. Always ensure that the ingredients you're using are safe for dogs. Avoid ingredients like raisins, chocolate, onions, and any artificial sweeteners like xylitol, as these can be toxic to dogs. And as always, treat your dog in moderation and consult with a veterinarian regarding any dietary changes or concerns.

Peanut Butter and Oat Biscuits

Ingredients:
- 1 1/2 cups whole wheat flour
- 1/2 cup rolled oats
- 1/4 cup dry milk
- 1/4 cup cornmeal
- 1/2 cup peanut butter (unsalted and without xylitol)
- 1/2 cup water
- 1 beaten egg

Directions:
1. Preheat oven to 350°F (175°C).
2. Mix flour, oats, dry milk, and cornmeal in a large bowl.
3. Add the peanut butter, water, and beaten egg. Mix well.
4. Roll out the dough on a floured surface and use cookie cutters to create shapes.
5. Place biscuits on a baking sheet and bake for 30 minutes.
6. Allow to cool completely before serving.

Apple and Carrot Crunchies

Ingredients:
- 2 cups whole wheat flour
- 1/2 cup rolled oats
- 1 apple, finely grated (seeded and cored)
- 1 carrot, finely grated
- 1 egg
- 1/3 cup water

Directions:
1. Preheat oven to 350°F (175°C).

2. In a large bowl, combine flour and oats.
3. Mix in the grated apple, carrot, egg, and water to form a dough.
4. Roll out dough and cut into desired shapes.
5. Place on a baking sheet and bake for 40 minutes.
6. Cool completely before serving.

Cheesy Dog Biscuits

Ingredients:
- 2 cups whole wheat flour
- 1 1/2 cups shredded cheddar cheese
- 1/2 cup milk
- 1/4 cup unsalted butter, melted
- 1 beaten egg

Directions:
1. Preheat oven to 375°F (190°C).
2. Mix all ingredients together in a bowl until a dough forms.
3. Roll out the dough on a floured surface and cut into desired shapes.
4. Place biscuits on a baking sheet and bake for 20 minutes or until lightly browned.
5. Allow to cool before serving.

Pumpkin and Cinnamon Treats

Ingredients:
- 2 1/2 cups whole wheat flour
- 1/2 cup 100% pure pumpkin puree (not pie filling)
- 1 egg
- 2 tablespoons coconut oil
- 1 teaspoon cinnamon

Directions:
1. Preheat oven to 350°F (175°C).
2. Mix all the ingredients in a bowl to form a dough.
3. Roll out the dough and cut into desired shapes.
4. Place treats on a baking sheet and bake for 30-35 minutes.
5. Cool completely before serving to your pup.

Soft Chews Recipes

Soft chews can be especially good for older dogs or dogs with dental issues. Always make sure the ingredients used are safe for dogs. It's best to introduce new treats gradually and in moderation. And, as always, consult with a veterinarian regarding any dietary changes or concerns.

Sweet Potato and Chicken Chews

Ingredients:
- 1 sweet potato, cooked and mashed
- 1 cup chicken breast, cooked and finely shredded
- 1 egg
- 2 tablespoons olive oil
- 1 tablespoon parsley, finely chopped (optional)

Directions:
1. Preheat oven to 325°F (165°C).
2. In a mixing bowl, combine the mashed sweet potato, shredded chicken, egg, olive oil, and parsley.
3. Mix until well combined.
4. Shape the mixture into small balls and place them on a lined baking sheet.
5. Flatten each ball slightly.
6. Bake for 15-20 minutes, or until they are firm but still soft to the touch.
7. Cool before serving.

Beef and Carrot Soft Bites

Ingredients:
- 1/2 pound ground beef
- 1 carrot, finely grated
- 1/2 cup oat flour (you can grind rolled oats in a blender)
- 1/4 cup beef broth or water
- 1 egg

Directions:
1. Preheat oven to 350°F (175°C).
2. In a skillet, cook the ground beef until fully browned.
3. In a bowl, mix the cooked beef, grated carrot, oat flour, broth, and egg.
4. Form the mixture into small patties and place on a lined baking sheet.
5. Bake for 15-18 minutes, ensuring they remain soft.
6. Let them cool before serving.

Peanut Butter and Banana Softies

Ingredients:
- 1 ripe banana, mashed
- 1/2 cup peanut butter (unsalted and without xylitol)
- 1 cup oat flour
- 1/4 cup plain yogurt

Directions:
1. Preheat oven to 350°F (175°C).
2. In a bowl, mix together the mashed banana, peanut butter, oat flour, and yogurt until smooth.
3. Drop spoonfuls of the mixture onto a lined baking sheet.
4. Flatten each spoonful slightly.
5. Bake for 12-15 minutes, ensuring the treats remain soft.
6. Cool before serving.

Salmon and Spinach Soft Chews

Ingredients:
- 1 can (6 oz) pink salmon in water, drained and flaked
- 1 cup fresh spinach, finely chopped
- 1 egg
- 1/2 cup oat flour
- 2 tablespoons olive oil

Directions:
1. Preheat oven to 325°F (165°C).
2. In a mixing bowl, combine flaked salmon, spinach, egg, oat flour, and olive oil.
3. Form the mixture into small balls and place on a lined baking sheet.
4. Flatten each ball slightly.
5. Bake for 12-15 minutes, ensuring they remain soft.
6. Let them cool before serving.

Frozen Delight Recipes

Frozen treats can be a refreshing way for dogs to cool down on a hot day. Always ensure that the ingredients you're using are safe for dogs. Remember to introduce new treats slowly and in moderation. And as always, consult with a veterinarian regarding any dietary changes or concerns.

Peanut Butter and Banana Pupsicles

Ingredients:
- 2 ripe bananas, mashed
- 1/2 cup peanut butter (unsalted and without xylitol)
- 1/4 cup water

Directions:
1. In a blender or food processor, combine the mashed bananas, peanut butter, and water.
2. Blend until smooth.
3. Pour the mixture into ice cube trays or silicone molds.
4. Freeze for 4-6 hours or until solid.
5. Remove from molds and serve to your pup.

Coconut and Blueberry Drops

Ingredients:
- 1 can (13.5 oz) coconut milk (unsweetened)
- 1 cup blueberries

Directions:
1. In a blender, combine coconut milk and blueberries until smooth.
2. Pour the mixture into ice cube trays or silicone molds.
3. Freeze for 4-6 hours or until solid.
4. Pop out the frozen treats and let your dog enjoy!

Chicken Broth and Veggie Cubes

Ingredients:
- 2 cups low-sodium chicken broth
- 1/2 cup finely chopped carrots
- 1/2 cup finely chopped green beans

Directions:
1. Mix together chicken broth, chopped carrots, and green beans in a bowl.
2. Pour the mixture into ice cube trays or silicone molds.
3. Freeze for 4-6 hours or until solid.
4. Serve these savory ice cubes as a chilly snack.

Pumpkin and Yogurt Creamsicles

Ingredients:

- 1 cup 100% pure pumpkin puree (not pie filling)
- 1 cup plain yogurt (unsweetened)
- 1 tablespoon honey (optional)

Directions:

1. In a bowl, mix together pumpkin puree, yogurt, and honey.
2. Pour the mixture into ice cube trays or silicone molds.
3. Freeze for 4-6 hours or until solid.
4. Unmold and give your dog a creamy, frozen delight.

Dehydrated Snacks

Dehydrated treats are a fantastic way to provide your dog with natural, preservative-free snacks. Always ensure the ingredients used are safe for dogs. Dehydrating times can vary based on the thickness of your slices and the specific dehydrator you use. It's important to make sure treats are fully dried to prevent mold. Always store dehydrated treats in a cool, dry place, and monitor their condition for safety. As always, consult with a veterinarian regarding any dietary changes or concerns.

Beef Liver Bites

Ingredients:
- 1 pound beef liver, sliced thin

Directions:
1. Rinse and pat dry the beef liver slices.
2. Arrange the slices in a single layer on the dehydrator trays.
3. Dehydrate at 140°F (60°C) for 6-8 hours or until completely dry and crisp.
4. Store in an airtight container in a cool, dark place.

Sweet Potato Chews

Ingredients:
- 2-3 large, sweet potatoes, washed

Directions:
1. Slice the sweet potatoes thinly, about 1/8-inch thick.
2. Arrange the slices in a single layer on the dehydrator trays.
3. Dehydrate at 125°F (52°C) for 6-8 hours or until they have a chewy texture.
4. For crispier treats, dehydrate for an additional 2-4 hours.
5. Store in an airtight container.

Chicken Jerky Strips(Dehydrated)

Ingredients:
- 2 boneless, skinless chicken breasts

Directions:
1. Trim any excess fat from the chicken breasts.
2. Slice the chicken into thin strips, about 1/4-inch thick.
3. Arrange the strips in a single layer on the dehydrator trays.
4. Dehydrate at 145°F (63°C) for 6-8 hours or until fully dried and easy to snap.
5. Store in an airtight container in the refrigerator.

Apple and Cinnamon Rings

Ingredients:
- 4 large apples, cored and sliced into rings
- 1 teaspoon ground cinnamon (optional)

Directions:
1. If using, sprinkle cinnamon over apple rings.
2. Arrange the apple rings in a single layer on the dehydrator trays.
3. Dehydrate at 135°F (57°C) for 6-8 hours or until fully dried and crisp.
4. Store in an airtight container.

Cultural or World Cuisine Inspired

Asian-Inspired Recipes

Always ensure ingredients are safe for dogs. These recipes are inspired by Asian cuisine but are adapted to be dog-safe. Always avoid ingredients like onions, garlic, and excessive salt, which can be harmful to dogs. As with any dietary changes or introductions, consult with a veterinarian and monitor your dog for any adverse reactions.

Chicken and Ginger Congee

Ingredients:
- 1 cup rice
- 4 cups low-sodium chicken broth
- 1 boneless, skinless chicken breast, diced
- 1 small piece of ginger, minced
- 1/2 cup chopped carrots
- 1/2 cup chopped green beans

Directions:
1. In a pot, combine rice, chicken broth, ginger, and diced chicken.
2. Bring to a boil, then reduce to a simmer and cover.
3. Allow to simmer for 1 hour, stirring occasionally.
4. Add carrots and green beans in the last 20 minutes of cooking.
5. Once cooked, let cool before serving to your dog.

Tofu and Vegetable Stir-Fry

Ingredients:
- 1 cup firm tofu, cubed
- 1 cup mixed vegetables (broccoli, bell peppers, snap peas)
- 2 teaspoons coconut oil
- 1 tablespoon low-sodium soy sauce (or tamari for gluten-free)

Directions:
1. In a skillet or wok, heat coconut oil.
2. Add tofu cubes and stir-fry until golden brown.
3. Add the vegetables and stir-fry for another 5 minutes or until just tender.

4. Drizzle with low-sodium soy sauce and mix well.
5. Allow to cool before serving.

Fish and Seaweed Broth

Ingredients:
- 2 fillets of white fish (e.g., cod, tilapia)
- 4 cups of water
- 1 sheet of nori seaweed, torn into small pieces
- 1/2 cup finely sliced zucchini

Directions:
1. In a pot, bring water to a boil.
2. Add fish fillets and reduce to a simmer.
3. Cook for about 10 minutes or until the fish is fully cooked and easily flakes.
4. Add zucchini slices and cook for another 5 minutes.
5. Turn off the heat and add nori seaweed.
6. Allow to cool before serving.

Bok Choy and Beef Medley

Ingredients:
- 1/2 pound lean beef, diced
- 2 bok choy heads, chopped
- 2 teaspoons sesame oil
- 1/2 cup cooked quinoa or rice

Directions:
1. In a skillet, heat sesame oil.
2. Add diced beef and cook until browned.
3. Add chopped bok choy and sauté until wilted.
4. Stir in the cooked quinoa or rice.
5. Remove from heat and let cool before serving.

Mediterranean-Inspired Recipes

Remember that dogs have different dietary needs and sensitivities. The following recipes are inspired by Mediterranean flavors but are made to be dog-friendly. Always avoid ingredients like onions, garlic, grapes, raisins, and excessive salt, which can be harmful to dogs. Before making any changes to your dog's diet or trying new ingredients, consult with a veterinarian.

Olive Oil and Herb Chicken

Ingredients:
- 2 boneless, skinless chicken breasts
- 1 tablespoon extra-virgin olive oil
- A pinch of dried rosemary and thyme
- 1/2 cup diced tomatoes (ensure no onions or garlic added)
- 1/2 cup cooked quinoa

Directions:
1. Heat olive oil in a skillet over medium heat.
2. Add chicken breasts and sprinkle with rosemary and thyme.
3. Cook until chicken is fully done, turning occasionally.
4. Add the diced tomatoes and cooked quinoa, stirring well.
5. Remove from heat, let it cool, then serve.

Lamb and Cucumber Salad

Ingredients:
- 1/2 pound ground lamb
- 1/2 cucumber, diced
- 1/2 red bell pepper, diced
- 1 tablespoon olive oil
- 1/2 cup cooked barley

Directions:
1. In a skillet, heat olive oil and cook ground lamb until browned.
2. In a mixing bowl, combine cooked lamb, cucumber, red bell pepper, and cooked barley.
3. Stir well to mix, let it cool, then serve.

Fish and Spinach Stew

Ingredients:
- 2 fillets of white fish (e.g., cod, tilapia)
- 2 cups spinach, chopped
- 2 cups low-sodium vegetable broth
- 1/2 cup diced carrots
- 1 tablespoon olive oil

Directions:
1. In a pot, heat olive oil and add the fish fillets. Cook until they start to flake.
2. Add vegetable broth and bring to a simmer.
3. Add carrots and simmer for 10 minutes.

4. Add chopped spinach and cook for another 5 minutes.
5. Remove from heat, let it cool, then serve.

Eggplant and Beef Casserole

Ingredients:
- 1/2 pound lean beef, diced
- 1 small eggplant, cubed
- 1 zucchini, sliced
- 1 tablespoon olive oil
- 1/2 cup cooked brown rice

Directions:
1. Preheat oven to 375°F (190°C).
2. In a skillet, heat olive oil and brown the beef.
3. In a baking dish, layer beef, eggplant cubes, and zucchini slices.
4. Top with cooked brown rice and a drizzle of olive oil.
5. Cover with aluminum foil and bake for 25 minutes.
6. Remove from oven, let it cool, then serve.

Latin American-Inspired Recipes

Dogs have specific dietary needs, so always ensure the ingredients are safe for them. These recipes reflect Latin American flavors but are adapted to be dog-friendly. Avoid ingredients like onions, garlic, avocados, and excessive spices, which can be harmful to dogs. As always, consult with a veterinarian when introducing new foods to your dog's diet and observe for any adverse reactions.

Chicken and Rice Arroz con Pollo

Ingredients:
- 2 boneless, skinless chicken breasts, diced
- 1 cup cooked brown rice
- 1 tablespoon olive oil
- 1/2 cup diced bell peppers (varied colors)
- 1/2 cup cooked black beans (ensure no seasoning or salt added)

Directions:
1. In a skillet, heat olive oil and cook the chicken pieces until fully done.
2. Add the bell peppers and stir-fry until slightly softened.
3. Mix in the cooked brown rice and black beans.
4. Once well-mixed and heated through, remove from the heat, let it cool, then serve.

Beef and Corn Empanada Filling

Ingredients:
- 1/2 pound lean ground beef
- 1/2 cup corn kernels (either fresh or frozen)
- 1 tablespoon olive oil
- 1/2 cup diced tomatoes (ensure no onions or garlic added)
- A pinch of cilantro, finely chopped

Directions:
1. In a skillet, heat olive oil and brown the ground beef.
2. Add the corn and diced tomatoes, mixing well.
3. Cook until heated through and well combined.
4. Sprinkle with a bit of cilantro for added flavor.
5. Once cool, serve as a delicious meal filling.

Fish and Quinoa Ceviche (Cooked Version)

Ingredients:
- 2 fillets of white fish (e.g., cod, tilapia)
- 1 cup cooked quinoa
- 1/2 cucumber, finely diced
- 1/2 bell pepper, finely diced
- Juice of 1 lime
- 1 tablespoon olive oil

Directions:
1. In a skillet, heat olive oil and cook the fish fillets until fully done.

2. In a mixing bowl, flake the cooked fish and combine with cooked quinoa, cucumber, and bell pepper.
3. Drizzle with lime juice and mix well.
4. Allow to cool before serving.

Tropical Fruit Salad

Ingredients:
- 1/2 cup diced pineapple
- 1/2 cup diced papaya
- 1/2 cup diced mango
- 1/2 cup cooked quinoa
- A splash of coconut milk

Directions:
1. In a bowl, mix together the diced fruits.
2. Add the cooked quinoa and mix well.
3. Drizzle with a bit of coconut milk for added flavor and moisture.
4. Let it cool, then serve as a refreshing treat or meal topper.

Classic American Classic Recipes

These recipes reflect classic American dishes, but they've been adapted to be dog-friendly. Always ensure that the ingredients are safe for your pet. Some human foods, like onions, garlic, grapes, raisins, chocolate, and certain sweeteners (like xylitol), can be toxic to dogs. Before making any changes to your dog's diet or trying new ingredients, always consult with a veterinarian.

Dog-Friendly Meatloaf

Ingredients:
- 1 pound lean ground beef or turkey
- 1 egg
- 1/2 cup oatmeal
- 1/2 cup diced carrots
- 1/2 cup peas

Directions:
1. Preheat oven to 375°F (190°C).
2. Mix together all the ingredients in a bowl.
3. Press the mixture into a loaf pan.
4. Bake for 40-45 minutes.
5. Let it cool before slicing and serving.

Pooch's Peanut Butter and Banana Sandwich

Ingredients:
- 2 slices of whole wheat bread
- 1 tablespoon peanut butter (ensure it doesn't contain xylitol)
- 1 banana, sliced

Directions:
1. Spread peanut butter on one slice of bread.
2. Place banana slices over the peanut butter.
3. Top with the second slice of bread.
4. Cut into manageable squares or triangles and serve.

Chicken Pot Pie Filling

Ingredients:
- 1 boneless, skinless chicken breast, diced
- 1/2 cup peas
- 1/2 cup diced carrots
- 1 cup low-sodium chicken broth
- 1 tablespoon olive oil

Directions:
1. In a skillet, heat the olive oil and cook the chicken until fully done.
2. Add the peas and carrots, then pour in the chicken broth.
3. Let simmer until the vegetables are tender.
4. Allow to cool and serve as a hearty meal or topping.

Bacon and Egg Breakfast Scramble

Ingredients:
- 2 eggs, beaten
- 2 strips of low-sodium bacon, cooked and crumbled
- 1/2 cup diced bell peppers
- 1/2 cup cooked quinoa

Directions:
1. In a skillet, scramble the eggs.
2. Once the eggs start to set, add the crumbled bacon and bell peppers.
3. Stir in the quinoa and mix until well combined.
4. Remove from heat, let it cool, and serve as a special breakfast treat.

Seasonal

Summer Cool-Down Recipes

Summer treats are a fantastic way to help your dog cool down, but always supervise when offering frozen goodies to ensure they don't swallow large pieces whole. Always consult with a vet before introducing new foods into your dog's diet.

Peanut Butter and Banana Creamsicles

Ingredients:
- 2 ripe bananas, mashed
- 1/2 cup peanut butter (ensure it doesn't contain xylitol)
- 1 cup plain yogurt

Directions:
1. Mix the mashed bananas, peanut butter, and yogurt in a bowl until smooth.
2. Pour the mixture into silicone molds or ice cube trays.
3. Freeze for several hours until solid.
4. Pop them out and serve as a delightful summer treat.

Berry Delight Frozen Cubes

Ingredients:
- 1 cup blueberries
- 1 cup strawberries, chopped
- 2 cups water or unsweetened coconut water

Directions:
1. Place a few blueberries and a piece of strawberry in each compartment of an ice cube tray.
2. Fill the compartments with water or coconut water.
3. Freeze until solid.
4. Serve the fruity cubes as a refreshing and hydrating snack.

Pup's Watermelon Sorbet

Ingredients:
- 2 cups seedless watermelon, cubed

- 1/2 cup coconut milk

Directions:

1. Blend the watermelon cubes in a blender or food processor until smooth.
2. Add coconut milk and blend until well combined.
3. Pour the mixture into a freezer-safe container and freeze for several hours.
4. Use a scoop to serve a refreshing dollop to your pup.

Chicken and Veggie Ice Treats

Ingredients:

- 1 cup low-sodium chicken broth
- 1/2 cup cooked and shredded chicken
- 1/2 cup finely chopped carrots
- 1/2 cup finely chopped cucumber

Directions:

1. In a mixing bowl, combine the chicken, carrots, and cucumber.
2. Divide the mixture among the compartments of an ice cube tray.
3. Carefully pour chicken broth over the mixture in each compartment.
4. Freeze until solid.
5. Pop them out and offer them as a savory, icy snack.

Autumn Warm-Up Recipes

Always ensure that the food cools down to a safe temperature before serving it to your dog. Remember, some human foods, like onions, garlic, grapes, raisins, and certain sweeteners (like xylitol), can be toxic to dogs. Always check the ingredients and consult with a veterinarian before introducing new foods into your dog's diet.

Hearty Chicken and Pumpkin Stew

Ingredients:
- 2 boneless, skinless chicken breasts, diced
- 1 cup pumpkin puree (not pie filling)
- 1/2 cup carrots, diced
- 1/2 cup green beans, chopped
- 2 cups low-sodium chicken broth
- 1 tablespoon olive oil

Directions:
1. In a pot, heat the olive oil and brown the chicken pieces.
2. Add carrots, green beans, and chicken broth. Bring to a simmer.
3. Once the vegetables are tender, stir in the pumpkin puree.
4. Simmer for an additional 10 minutes, then let it cool before serving.

Beef and Sweet Potato Mash

Ingredients:
- 1 pound lean ground beef
- 1 large, sweet potato, peeled and cubed
- 1/2 cup peas
- 1 tablespoon olive oil

Directions:
1. In a skillet, heat the olive oil and brown the ground beef. Remove the beef and set it aside.
2. In the same skillet, add the sweet potato cubes and a little water. Cover and let them steam until tender.
3. Mash the sweet potatoes, then mix in the beef and peas. Serve warm.

Apple and Oat Warm Porridge

Ingredients:
- 1 apple, peeled, cored, and diced
- 1 cup rolled oats
- 2 cups water
- 1/4 teaspoon cinnamon (optional)

Directions:
1. In a pot, bring water to a boil and add the oats.
2. Reduce heat and simmer, stirring occasionally until the oats are cooked.
3. Add the apples and cinnamon, cooking for an additional 5 minutes.
4. Allow to cool to a safe temperature before serving.

Turkey and Cranberry Comfort

Ingredients:
- 1 pound ground turkey
- 1/4 cup cranberries (ensure they are unsweetened and plain)
- 1 zucchini, diced
- 1 tablespoon olive oil

Directions:
1. In a skillet, heat the olive oil and cook the ground turkey until fully browned.
2. Add the zucchini and cranberries, cooking until the zucchini is tender.
3. Serve this comforting mix warm.

Winter Comfort Recipes

Always cool down the food to a safe temperature before serving. It's crucial to remember that certain human foods are toxic to dogs. Always consult with a veterinarian before introducing new foods to your dog's diet.

Hearty Beef and Vegetable Soup

Ingredients:
- 1 pound lean beef stew meat, diced
- 2 carrots, sliced
- 1/2 cup green beans, chopped
- 1/2 cup peas
- 3 cups low-sodium beef or vegetable broth
- 1 tablespoon olive oil

Directions:
1. In a pot, heat the olive oil and brown the beef stew meat.
2. Add carrots, green beans, peas, and broth. Simmer until the meat is tender and the vegetables are cooked.
3. Let the soup cool to a safe temperature before serving.

Wholesome Chicken and Rice

Ingredients:
- 2 boneless, skinless chicken breasts
- 1 cup brown rice
- 2 1/2 cups water
- 1/2 cup broccoli florets, chopped

Directions:
1. In a pot, add chicken breasts, rice, and water. Bring to a boil.
2. Reduce heat to a simmer and cook covered until the rice is tender and the chicken is fully cooked.
3. Add the broccoli florets in the last 10 minutes of cooking.
4. Once done, shred the chicken inside the pot, stir, and serve when cooled.

Lamb and Quinoa Warm Bowl

Ingredients:
- 1 pound ground lamb
- 1 cup quinoa, rinsed
- 2 cups low-sodium vegetable broth
- 1 zucchini, diced

Directions:
1. In a skillet, brown the ground lamb. Remove excess fat.
2. In a separate pot, cook quinoa in vegetable broth according to package instructions.
3. Once quinoa is cooked, mix in the lamb and zucchini. Cover and let the warmth steam the zucchini until tender.
4. Let it cool to a safe temperature and serve.

Turkey and Barley Stew

Ingredients:
- 1 pound ground turkey
- 1/2 cup barley
- 2 1/2 cups low-sodium chicken broth
- 1 carrot, diced
- 1/2 cup chopped spinach

Directions:
1. In a skillet, cook the ground turkey until browned.
2. In a pot, bring chicken broth to a boil and add barley. Simmer until the barley is halfway cooked.
3. Add the cooked turkey and diced carrots to the pot. Continue simmering until the barley is fully cooked and the carrots are tender.
4. Stir in the chopped spinach just before serving, allowing it to wilt from the stew's warmth.
5. Allow the stew to cool before offering it to your furry friend.

Spring Freshness Recipes

Always ensure the dishes are cooled to a safe temperature before serving. It's essential to remember that certain ingredients might not be suitable for all dogs, so always consult with a veterinarian before introducing new foods to your dog's diet.

Chicken and Garden Vegetable Bowl

Ingredients:
- 2 boneless, skinless chicken breasts
- 1 cup snap peas, chopped
- 1 carrot, grated
- 1/2 cup cooked quinoa
- 1 tablespoon olive oil

Directions:
1. In a skillet, heat the olive oil and cook the chicken breasts until fully cooked. Once done, dice or shred the chicken.
2. Combine the chicken, snap peas, carrot, and quinoa in a bowl, tossing them together.
3. Serve cool or at room temperature.

Salmon and Fresh Herbs Salad

Ingredients:
- 1 fillet of salmon
- 1/2 cup cooked couscous
- 1 tablespoon fresh parsley, finely chopped
- 1 tablespoon fresh dill, finely chopped
- A squeeze of lemon juice

Directions:
1. Grill or bake the salmon fillet until fully cooked. Flake the salmon into small pieces.
2. In a bowl, mix the flaked salmon, couscous, parsley, and dill.
3. Drizzle with a little lemon juice for added freshness.
4. Allow to cool and serve.

Turkey and Spring Greens

Ingredients:
- 1 pound ground turkey
- 1 cup chopped spinach
- 1/2 cup blueberries
- 1 tablespoon flaxseed oil

Directions:
1. In a skillet, cook the ground turkey until browned and fully cooked.
2. Allow the turkey to cool a bit, then mix in the chopped spinach. The residual heat will lightly wilt the spinach.
3. Add the blueberries and drizzle with flaxseed oil for an omega boost.
4. Serve at room temperature.

Lamb and Mint Refreshment

Ingredients:
- 1 pound ground lamb
- 1 zucchini, spiralized or thinly sliced
- A few fresh mint leaves, finely chopped
- 1 tablespoon olive oil

Directions:
1. In a skillet, brown the ground lamb. Remove from heat and let it cool.
2. Mix in the spiralized zucchini, ensuring a good mix of lamb and zucchini in every bite.
3. Sprinkle with fresh mint and drizzle with olive oil.
4. Serve this refreshing dish at room temperature.

Advanced or Gourmet

Special Occasion Recipes

Always ensure the ingredients are safe for dogs and do not contain harmful additives. Remember that some ingredients, even those suitable for humans, can be harmful to dogs. Always consult with a veterinarian regarding dietary changes and special treats.

Gourmet Beef and Vegetable Terrine

Ingredients:
- 1 pound lean ground beef
- 1/2 cup finely chopped spinach
- 1/4 cup grated zucchini
- 1/4 cup grated carrots
- 1/4 cup peas
- 1 egg
- 2 tablespoons parsley, chopped

Directions:
1. Preheat the oven to 350°F (175°C).
2. In a mixing bowl, combine all the ingredients and mix thoroughly.
3. Press the mixture into a loaf pan.
4. Bake for about 40 minutes or until cooked through.
5. Allow to cool and then slice into portions. Garnish with a sprinkle of parsley before serving.

Tuna and Sweet Potato Cakes

Ingredients:
- 1 can of tuna in water, drained
- 1 sweet potato, boiled and mashed
- 1 egg
- 1/4 cup finely chopped parsley
- 2 tablespoons coconut flour

Directions:
1. In a bowl, combine the tuna, mashed sweet potato, egg, parsley, and coconut flour.
2. Shape the mixture into small patties.
3. Cook the patties in a non-stick skillet over medium heat until golden brown on each side.

4. Allow to cool and serve garnished with additional parsley.

Pumpkin and Blueberry Dog Cake

Ingredients:
- 1/2 cup pumpkin puree
- 1/4 cup coconut oil, melted
- 2 eggs
- 1 cup almond flour
- 1/4 cup blueberries
- 1 teaspoon baking powder

Directions:
1. Preheat oven to 350°F (175°C).
2. In a mixing bowl, whisk together pumpkin puree, melted coconut oil, and eggs.
3. Gradually fold in the almond flour and baking powder until the mixture is smooth.
4. Gently fold in the blueberries.
5. Pour the batter into a greased cake pan and bake for about 25 minutes or until a toothpick comes out clean.
6. Allow the cake to cool before serving. For an added touch, spread a thin layer of plain Greek yogurt on top as "frosting."

Chicken and Apple Stuffed Bell Peppers

Ingredients:
- 2 large bell peppers (any color)
- 1/2 pound ground chicken
- 1 apple, finely diced
- 1/4 cup cooked quinoa
- 1/4 cup peas
- A sprinkle of turmeric and parsley

Directions:
1. Preheat the oven to 350°F (175°C).
2. Cut the tops off the bell peppers and remove the seeds.
3. In a skillet, cook the ground chicken until fully browned.
4. Add the diced apple, cooked quinoa, and peas to the skillet, stirring until well combined.
5. Stuff the bell peppers with the chicken mixture.
6. Place the stuffed peppers in a baking dish and bake for about 30 minutes or until the peppers are tender.
7. Allow to cool slightly before serving. Sprinkle with turmeric and parsley for added health benefits and garnish.

Multi-Step or Time-Intensive

Recipes

As always, ensure that all the ingredients used are safe for canine consumption and free from harmful additives or seasonings. Before making dietary changes or introducing gourmet meals, consult with a veterinarian.

Braised Beef and Barley Stew

Ingredients:
- 1 pound beef chunks (suitable for stewing)
- 1 cup pearl barley
- 2 cups beef broth (low sodium)
- 1/2 cup chopped carrots
- 1/2 cup chopped green beans
- 2 tablespoons olive oil
- Fresh parsley for garnish

Directions:
1. In a pot, heat the olive oil and brown the beef chunks on all sides.
2. Add the beef broth and bring to a simmer.
3. Cover and let it cook on low heat for an hour.
4. Add the pearl barley, carrots, and green beans.
5. Continue cooking for another hour, or until the beef is tender and the barley is cooked through.
6. Allow to cool slightly, garnish with fresh parsley, and serve.

Homemade Chicken Jerky

Ingredients:
- 2 boneless, skinless chicken breasts

Directions:
1. Preheat your oven to 170°F (75°C) or the lowest setting.
2. Clean the chicken breasts and remove any fat.
3. Slice the chicken breasts into thin strips, about 1/4 inch thick.
4. Place the strips on a baking sheet lined with parchment paper, ensuring they don't overlap.
5. Bake for 2 to 3 hours, flipping the strips halfway through, until they are dried and hardened.
6. Allow them to cool before serving. Store in an airtight container.

Slow-Cooked Lamb and Vegetable Medley

Ingredients:
- 1 pound lamb, cut into chunks
- 1/2 cup chopped zucchini
- 1/2 cup chopped sweet potatoes

- 1/4 cup green peas
- 1/4 cup chopped carrots
- 2 cups water or low sodium broth
- Fresh mint for garnish

Directions:

1. Place the lamb chunks in a slow cooker.
2. Add the vegetables and water or broth.
3. Set the slow cooker on low and let it cook for 6-8 hours.
4. Once done, let it cool slightly. Garnish with fresh mint leaves before serving.

Quinoa and Salmon Cakes

Ingredients:

- 1 cup cooked quinoa
- 1/2 pound salmon fillet, cooked and flaked
- 1 egg
- 2 tablespoons finely chopped parsley
- 1 tablespoon coconut oil or olive oil

Directions:

1. In a mixing bowl, combine the cooked quinoa, flaked salmon, egg, and parsley.
2. Shape the mixture into small patties.
3. Heat the oil in a skillet over medium heat.
4. Cook the patties for about 3-4 minutes on each side, or until they're golden brown and cooked through.
5. Allow the cakes to cool down a bit before serving to your dog.

Homemade Supplements and Mix-Ins

Bone Broth Recipes

When serving, always ensure the broth is at an appropriate temperature for your dog. Bone broth can be poured over regular dog food or given separately as a liquid treat or supplement. Before incorporating new food items into your dog's diet regularly, consult with a veterinarian.

Basic Chicken Bone Broth

Ingredients:
- 2-3 pounds of chicken bones (necks, backs, wings, or a combination)
- 2 tablespoons apple cider vinegar
- 4-5 cups of water (or enough to cover the bones)
- Optional: carrots, celery, or parsley for added nutrition

Directions:
1. Place the chicken bones in a large pot or slow cooker.
2. Add the apple cider vinegar and water.
3. If using, add the optional vegetables.
4. Bring the mixture to a simmer over low heat.
5. Cover and continue simmering for 12-24 hours.
6. Allow to cool and strain to remove bones and vegetables.
7. Store in the refrigerator or freezer for longer storage.

Beef Marrow Bone Broth

Ingredients:
- 2-3 pounds beef marrow bones
- 2 tablespoons apple cider vinegar
- 5-6 cups of water
- Optional: chopped vegetables like carrots, celery, and green beans

Directions:
1. Roast the beef marrow bones in the oven at 400°F for 30 minutes to enhance flavor.
2. Place the roasted bones in a pot or slow cooker.
3. Add the apple cider vinegar, water, and optional vegetables.

4. Bring to a simmer over low heat.
5. Cover and continue simmering for 24-48 hours.
6. Cool and strain to remove bones and vegetables.
7. Store as indicated in the chicken broth recipe.

Turkey and Ginger Bone Broth

Ingredients:
- 2-3 pounds turkey bones
- 2 tablespoons apple cider vinegar
- 1-inch piece of fresh ginger, sliced
- 5-6 cups of water

Directions:
1. Place turkey bones in a pot or slow cooker.
2. Add the apple cider vinegar, ginger slices, and water.
3. Simmer over low heat, covered, for 24 hours.
4. Cool, then strain to remove bones and ginger.
5. Store as indicated in the chicken broth recipe.

Fish Bone Broth

Ingredients:
- Fish heads and bones from non-oily fish (like cod or halibut)
- 2 tablespoons apple cider vinegar
- 1-2 seaweed sheets (like kombu or nori)
- 4-5 cups of water

Directions:
1. Place fish heads and bones in a pot.
2. Add the apple cider vinegar, seaweed sheets, and water.
3. Bring to a simmer over low heat.
4. Cover and simmer for 4-6 hours.
5. Allow to cool and then strain.
6. Store as indicated in the chicken broth recipe.

Herbal Supplement Recipes

It's essential to start with small amounts when introducing any new supplement and monitor your dog for any adverse reactions.

Chamomile and Lavender Calming Blend

Ingredients:
- 2 tablespoons dried chamomile flowers
- 1 tablespoon dried lavender flowers
- 2 cups boiling water

Directions:
1. In a heat-safe bowl, combine chamomile and lavender.
2. Pour boiling water over the herbs.
3. Allow the mixture to steep for 10-15 minutes.
4. Strain and let it cool.
5. Offer 1-2 tablespoons to your dog, adding it to their food or water. Store the remaining blend in the refrigerator.

Benefits: Chamomile and lavender are known for their calming properties, making this blend suitable for anxious dogs or for times of increased stress.

Minty Fresh Breath Supplement

Ingredients:
- A handful of fresh parsley
- A handful of fresh mint leaves
- 2 cups water

Directions:
1. Place parsley and mint leaves in a blender.
2. Add water and blend until smooth.
3. Pour the blend into ice cube trays and freeze.
4. Give your dog one cube a day to freshen breath.

Benefits: Parsley and mint are natural breath fresheners. This supplement can support oral health and give your dog a refreshing treat.

Turmeric and Black Pepper Joint Health Supplement

Ingredients:
- 1/4 cup turmeric powder
- 1/2 teaspoon freshly ground black pepper
- 1/2 cup water
- 1/4 cup coconut oil (melted)

Directions:
1. In a small pot, combine turmeric, black pepper, and water.
2. Heat gently, stirring continuously until it forms a thick paste.
3. Allow to cool slightly and then stir in the melted coconut oil.
4. Store in an airtight container in the refrigerator.

5. Add a small amount (1/2 teaspoon for small dogs, 1 teaspoon for medium dogs, 1-1 1/2 teaspoons for large dogs) to your dog's food daily.

Benefits: Turmeric and black pepper have anti-inflammatory properties that can support joint health. The coconut oil aids in absorption.

Rosemary Digestive Aid

Ingredients:
- 2 tablespoons dried rosemary leaves
- 2 cups boiling water

Directions:
1. Place the dried rosemary in a heat-safe bowl.
2. Pour boiling water over the rosemary.
3. Allow to steep for 10 minutes.
4. Strain and let cool.
5. Offer 1-2 tablespoons to your dog by adding it to their food or water. Store the remaining blend in the refrigerator.

Benefits: Rosemary can help in digestion and soothe an upset stomach.

Nut and Seed Butter Recipes

Remember, nuts and seeds should be unsalted, and it's important to avoid nuts that are toxic to dogs, such as macadamia nuts. These butters can be given in small amounts as a treat or used as a mix-in with their regular food. They're rich in healthy fats and can be a delightful addition to a dog's diet. Always monitor your dog for any allergies and ensure they're not given in excess.

Peanut Butter Delight

Ingredients:
- 2 cups unsalted, raw peanuts
- 1-2 tablespoons coconut oil (optional for smoother consistency)

Directions:
1. Preheat oven to 350°F (175°C).
2. Spread the peanuts on a baking sheet and roast for 10 minutes, stirring halfway.
3. Allow the peanuts to cool slightly.
4. Place the roasted peanuts in a food processor and blend until creamy, adding coconut oil as needed for desired consistency.
5. Store in an airtight container in the refrigerator.

Sunny Sunflower Seed Spread

Ingredients:
- 2 cups raw sunflower seeds
- 1-2 tablespoons coconut oil (optional for smoother consistency)

Directions:
1. In a skillet over medium heat, toast the sunflower seeds until golden brown, stirring frequently.
2. Let the seeds cool.
3. Transfer the toasted seeds to a food processor, blending until smooth, adding coconut oil as necessary.
4. Store in an airtight container in the fridge.

Flaxseed Butter Boost

Ingredients:
- 2 cups raw flaxseeds
- 1-2 tablespoons coconut oil

Directions:
1. Using a skillet over medium heat, toast the flaxseeds, stirring frequently, until they start to pop.
2. Remove from heat and allow to cool.
3. In a food processor, blend the toasted flaxseeds, adding coconut oil for desired consistency.
4. Store in a sealed container in the refrigerator.

Raw Foods

Safe Raw Meat Recipes

When preparing raw meals for dogs, it's essential to ensure that the meat is fresh and comes from a reliable source to minimize the risk of bacterial contamination. Remember, when serving raw foods, be mindful of cleanliness and wash all utensils, bowls, and surfaces thoroughly to prevent the spread of bacteria. Always observe your dog for any changes in behavior or digestive upset when introducing new foods. It's also a good idea to consult with a veterinarian or pet nutritionist to ensure your dog's dietary needs are being met.

Chicken and Veggie Medley (Raw)

Ingredients:
- 1 pound of boneless, skinless chicken breast, finely chopped
- 1 cup of grated carrots
- 1 cup of finely chopped spinach
- 1 tablespoon of fish oil
- 1/2 cup of blueberries

Directions:
1. In a large mixing bowl, combine the chicken, carrots, and spinach.
2. Stir in the fish oil to ensure an even coat.
3. Gently fold in the blueberries.
4. Serve in your dog's dish.

Beef Bliss Bowl

Ingredients:
- 1 pound of lean ground beef
- 1/2 cup of diced cucumber
- 1/4 cup of pumpkin puree
- 1/2 cup of chopped kale
- 1 tablespoon of flaxseed oil

Directions:
1. In a large bowl, mix together the ground beef, cucumber, and kale.
2. Stir in the pumpkin puree and flaxseed oil, mixing until everything is evenly combined.
3. Portion out the appropriate amount for your dog's size and serve.

Salmon Sensation

Ingredients:
- 1 pound of fresh salmon fillet, finely chopped
- 1/2 cup of zucchini noodles
- 1/2 cup of finely chopped broccoli
- 1 tablespoon of coconut oil
- A sprinkle of dried seaweed (ensure it's free from any additives)

Directions:
1. In a mixing bowl, combine the salmon, zucchini noodles, and broccoli.
2. Mix in the coconut oil.
3. Sprinkle the seaweed on top and stir until evenly distributed.
4. Serve immediately.

Turkey and Apple Toss

Ingredients:
- 1 pound of ground turkey
- 1 apple, cored and finely chopped (ensure no seeds)
- 1/2 cup of green beans, finely chopped
- 1 tablespoon of olive oil
- 1/4 teaspoon of turmeric powder (optional)

Directions:
1. Combine the ground turkey, apple chunks, and green beans in a large bowl.
2. Drizzle with olive oil and sprinkle with turmeric.
3. Mix everything together until well combined.
4. Dish out and serve.

Raw Mix-In Recipes

Raw mix-ins can be a great way to add fresh, whole-food nutrients to your dog's diet. Always introduce new foods gradually and monitor for any adverse reactions. If you're uncertain about any ingredient or quantity, consulting with a veterinarian or pet nutritionist is a wise step.

Berry Good Boost

Ingredients:
- 1/2 cup of blueberries
- 1/2 cup of strawberries, hulled and chopped
- 1 tablespoon of chia seeds
- 2 tablespoons of plain kefir

Directions:
1. In a bowl, mash the blueberries and strawberries together until they form a chunky puree.
2. Mix in the chia seeds and kefir until well combined.
3. Allow the mixture to sit for 10 minutes, giving time for the chia seeds to absorb some of the liquid.
4. Stir again before adding a few spoonfuls to your dog's meal.

Green Machine

Ingredients:
- 1 cup of spinach leaves
- 1/2 cup of chopped cucumber
- 1/2 an avocado, pitted and peeled
- A sprinkle of kelp powder

Directions:
1. Place the spinach, cucumber, and avocado in a blender or food processor.
2. Blend until smooth. If it's too thick, you can add a little water.
3. Transfer to a bowl and sprinkle with kelp powder.
4. Mix thoroughly and spoon a few tablespoons onto your dog's food.

Omega Mix

Ingredients:
- 1/4 cup of finely chopped raw salmon (ensure it's free from bones)
- 1 tablespoon of hemp seeds
- 1 tablespoon of flaxseed oil

Directions:
1. In a bowl, combine the chopped salmon and hemp seeds.
2. Drizzle with flaxseed oil and mix until well combined.
3. Add a tablespoon or two to your dog's meal for an omega-rich boost.

Tropical Digestive Helper

Ingredients:
- 1/2 cup of fresh pineapple, chopped
- 1/2 cup of fresh papaya, chopped
- 1 tablespoon of coconut oil
- 1 teaspoon of ginger paste

Directions:
1. In a blender, combine the pineapple, papaya, and ginger paste. Blend until smooth.
2. Transfer to a bowl and stir in the coconut oil.
3. Let it sit for a few minutes to allow the flavors to meld.
4. Spoon a small amount onto your dog's meal.

Conclusion: A Tail Wagging Journey to Health and Happiness

And here we are, dear readers, at the end of this delightful culinary journey. What an adventure it has been! From the basics of dog nutrition to adapting recipes to unique needs, and finally ensuring our furry pals are thriving—we've covered it all. But as the last page of this guide approaches, it's essential to understand that the journey of feeding our pets with love, attention, and awareness is never truly over. Instead, it's a continuous cycle of learning, adapting, and growing alongside our four-legged friends.

A Labor of Love

By now, it should be abundantly clear that homemade dog food is more than just mixing a few ingredients in a bowl—it's a labor of love. It's about taking that extra step to ensure our dogs aren't just eating but thriving. It's about the joy you feel when you see your dog's eyes light up at mealtime or the satisfaction of knowing you're giving them the best nutrition possible. Every scoop, every meal, every ingredient is a testament to the love and care you have for your canine companion.

The Power of Adaptation

One of the most significant lessons we've emphasized throughout this guide is the importance of adaptation. Dogs, much like humans, are ever-evolving. Their nutritional needs change with age, health conditions, and even the seasons. But armed with the knowledge you now possess, you can face these changes confidently, making necessary tweaks to their diet. Always remember to monitor, adjust, and consult professionals when in doubt.

Celebrate the Small Victories

Maybe your previously finicky eater now gobbles down meals with gusto, or perhaps your senior dog seems to have a renewed pep in their step. Maybe you've finally mastered that one recipe, or you've noticed your dog's coat becoming shinier. Whatever it might be, take a moment to celebrate these victories. Every positive change is a testament to the effort you've put in, and it's worth a moment of pride and joy.

The Community Awaits

One of the wonderful things about venturing into homemade dog food is the community that comes with it. All around the world, pet parents like you are embarking on similar journeys, sharing their stories, recipes, and experiences. Engage with them! Whether it's through online forums, social media, or local pet groups, there's a wealth of collective knowledge and camaraderie out there waiting for you.

Keep Learning

While this book aims to be a comprehensive guide, the world of dog nutrition is vast and ever-evolving. New research, findings, and trends emerge regularly. Stay curious and keep learning. Subscribe to pet nutrition journals, attend seminars, or read up on the latest research. The more you know, the better equipped you'll be to make informed decisions for your pet's well-being.

Gratitude and Reflection

Take a moment to reflect on this journey you've embarked on. It's no small feat to take the reins of your dog's nutrition, but you've done it with grace, dedication, and love. Be thankful for the wagging tails, the contented sighs after a good meal, and the wet-nosed nuzzles. These are the signs of a happy, well-fed dog and are the rewards for all your hard work.

Looking Ahead

So, what's next? Now that you're well-versed in the world of homemade dog food, the possibilities are endless. Perhaps you'll start growing some of your own dog-friendly veggies in a garden or delve deeper into creating specialized recipes for different breeds. Maybe you'll become an advocate, educating other pet parents about the benefits of homemade dog food. The sky's the limit!

A Final Word

As we wrap up this book, remember this: At the heart of every meal, every recipe, and every decision is love. The love you have for your dog, and the love they endlessly give back to you. It's this bond, this unwavering companionship, that makes all the efforts worthwhile.

Thank you for joining us on this journey. Here's to many more happy meals, wagging tails, and moments of joy with your furry friend. From our kitchen to yours, bon appétit and happy tails!

Spreading the Joy of Healthy Tails

Now that you've got all the tips and tricks for making healthy, homemade dog food, it's time to share your newfound knowledge with others. You can help fellow dog lovers discover how to whip up nutritious and delicious meals for their furry friends.

By leaving your honest review of this book on Amazon, you're guiding other pet parents to the resource they need. Your opinion matters a lot! It's not just about giving feedback; it's about guiding others who share your passion for ensuring the well-being of our four-legged family members.

Thank you sincerely for your assistance. The world of homemade dog food thrives on shared experiences and knowledge – and by leaving your review, you're playing a crucial part in this. You're not just helping me; you're helping countless dogs and their families find the path to better health and happiness.

SCAN BELOW TO LEAVE A REVIEW

With gratitude, Nora Howland

P.S. - Remember, sharing good things makes you an even better friend. If you love this book, spread the word!

Seasonal Dog Treats for Every Holiday

I'm so excited to offer you your bonus!!

A collection of homemade dog treat recipes tailored for various holidays and seasons. Each recipe blends tradition with dog-friendly ingredients, focusing on both delight and nutrition to ensure your canine companion enjoys the festivities safely. From Halloween pumpkins to Valentine's Day berries, this book is designed for bakers of all levels, emphasizing the joy of creating lasting memories with your pet. It's not just a recipe book, but a celebration of the special bond between dogs and their owners, ensuring your furry friend is part of every cherished holiday moment.

SCAN TO GET YOUR COPY NOW

PASTOR [illegible] REFLECTIONS — Part 6
April 1, 2018 — Ressurection Sunday

Disciples are conflicted with the Truth of the Gospel on what Jesus said — He is risen!

A new alignment, attunement + acceptance, a new assignment!

• When God gives you a new understanding you can't stay where you were!

• You can't keep doing what you're doing!

• Time for renewed action.

Hanging out at the tomb — Long Enough!

Jesus is alive + victorious

Time to get a NEW VISION!

CPSIA information can be obtained
at www.ICGtesting.com
Printed in the USA
FFOW04n1736260917
40375FF

9 781478 790129

for reviewing my work prior to publication and for helping me to spread news about Defined by Attitude: The Power of Positivity to the world. Last and certainly not least, I am thankful to all of the coaches, mentors, confidants, and authors who showed extreme transparency while sharing their writing and publishing stories with me.

Each of you have been a true inspiration and kept me moving forward to complete this writing. I could not have done it without you. Thank you for pouring so much into me. I dedicate this book to each of you.

Introduction

Are you ready to unleash the power of positivity into your life and change how you view the world and how the world views you? Are you ready to improve how you relate to others and make other lives better through your critical touch points? Are you ready to leap into a new world and claim your world-class positive attitude? If you answered yes to any or all of these questions, *Defined by Attitude: The Power of Positivity* is for you.

Throughout life, in my professional career, in my social and civic circles, and in personal relationships I have observed a few things about other people and about myself. We are unique and represent a diverse range of values, preferences, inclinations, and passions. There is a choice each of us makes that has a tremendous impact on how we progress down our life path. I have noticed there are few choices an individual makes in life that have a greater impact than the attitude that an individual chooses. Fortunately, caring individuals helped me understand the importance of developing and maintaining a positive approach to life. I have been coached and coach others regarding the value of leveraging positivity. Your attitude and your resulting approach to life can be a powerful ally or a detriment, depending on your choice. I am convinced that most personal and professional success models begin with a person's attitude. Conversely, the road to failure for many also begins with the attitude chosen or developed along the way.

Defined by Attitude was written to help you understand how you

present yourself to the world. My goal is for you to embrace the power of positivity today. The progression of events that start with your attitude can lead to some amazing outcomes. Additionally, my goal is to inspire you to reach higher and claim the world-class positive attitude that awaits you. You can do it, and I want to assist. This book is not a feel-good story based on a dreamy vision filled with repetitive "have-a-nice-day" type statements. While I do want every day for you to be outstanding in a positive way, the journey through life has plenty of bumps in the road that may keep each of us from being our best. Through leveraging the power of positivity, each of us becomes equipped to step into new territory in terms of how we present ourselves. After all, we do not control the majority of what happens around us or what happens to us. What we are able to control is how we react to those events. The power of positivity also enables each of us to prepare for future interactions and events, when we have the right attitude.

When I wrote *Defined by Attitude*, my goal was to create meaningful dialogue with you and encourage you to think about your attitude in a different way. If you are already in a positive place, then I challenge you to go further. The format provides introspective questions along the way called "Attitudinal Checkups" and positive affirmations at the conclusion of each chapter. Use these tools and challenge yourself to make the next steps.

As you begin this journey, remember you are defined by your attitude, so constantly ask yourself how you wish to be defined. Get ready, and commit to making a positive difference. The world is waiting. *Defined by Attitude: The Power of Positivity* is the first step toward transformation. I look forward to hearing from you later to let me know how you are applying your attitudinal superpowers. Be sure to contact me with stories of your progress by sending an email to info@infinityleadershipconsulting.org, subject line: DBA-My Journey.

CHAPTER 1

Your Attitude: What Is it, and What Is All the Fuss?

Continuous, positive improvement in the small parts of one's attitude makes a large impact in one's life.

It cannot be seen; however, you may wear it on your countenance. It cannot be placed in a box, though it can certainly "box" you into an undesirable place. It cannot fly, yet it can propel you to heights never seen and to experiences not yet encountered. Your physician will never detect it with an MRI or x-ray. At the same time, it serves as a catalyst to influence what you do and your approach to life and living. What is this all-important force that I describe? Surely any force with this much power and effect on us can neither be a mystery nor some little-known fact.

Life has become very complex. Many years ago, we began sending astronauts into outer space. People took great forward strides and introduced technological breakthroughs previously unheard of and unfathomed by the human mind. New medical techniques came about that made the unthinkable conceivable. Global communications now link us with individuals around the world in a manner as simple as making a phone call or accessing the Internet. Through the many layers of complexity and technology, there are some very

human traits that makes it all work and makes a difference in our daily lives.

This "thing" I wish to spend some time covering with you through my writing is your attitude. Given the title of this book, you probably already knew where I was going and what I referenced. This chapter, as an icebreaker, will take us into the attitude discussion and is the first step in understanding important facets and components that make up and affect attitudes. I will cover the *"so-what factor"* of your attitude. When we understand how attitudes operate and the dynamics of how various attitudes interact, lives can change for the better. When we fully capture the power of positivity and apply this concept daily, lives can change forever.

I captured my thoughts and will present them from a practical, everyday living perspective. I must make that declaration early, before you put this book aside or close your e-reader believing I am about to delve into a jargon-filled scientific discussion dealing with motivation theory, psychosis, the psyche, or anything along those paths. There are plenty of scholars, professionals, researchers, and writers available to deal with all of those areas on a scientific and technical level. Many of them have distinguished themselves by their amazing findings. I defer to those subject-matter experts for in-depth coverage of those areas. I wish to engage you in what I will call a *close-to-home* discussion dealing with attitude. Let us begin our dialogue.

Your attitude affects you and how you react to situations and events encountered throughout the majority of your life. I say the majority of one's life, because I believe that individuals must have the capacity to react to what happens to them with some level of willful consciousness; thus, one could argue that newborn children are limited in their ability to display or control their attitude. At the same time, we know it does not take very long for infants to develop a diverse range of expressions and reactions that are directly reflective of their feelings.

In many instances, we may not realize the effect of our attitude. We may miss or ignore the impact attitude has on our lives. How

many times has something happened to you and later, in a quiet moment, you sat down to reflect on how you felt in retrospect? How many times have you been caught up between something wonderful and something unpleasant, which compelled you to react in a certain way? Even when contemplating a future event or experience, you may approach it in a certain way with specific expectations of what may happen or what you think will take place. Those moments and reflections are what give our lives flavor. One could refer to these moments as the spice of life. These are the thoughts and feelings that may cause us to care and may render us emotionally hooked to a person, cause, or situation. Left unchecked, these thoughts may have the potential to cause us to become emotionally detached, distant, or resentful. I could continue with myriad scenarios of life's situations and events. The common filter, which is the lens for your approach to your life and everything within it, is your attitude.

Your attitude is part of what makes your experience on this earth unique. That is not such a profound thought in isolation, so I will continue. We know we have an individual approach to and interpretation of life. While I understand and believe in certain group dynamics, no group of individuals or the composing members are the same. Diverse personalities, varied experiences, and the simple fact that not everyone likes or dislikes the same things in the same way, make us different. There is great power and value in recognizing and maximizing the differences that exist between and among people and cultures.

I will illustrate my point using an example that may resonate with you. Occasionally we may enjoy a between-meal snack of something either healthy or pleasurable. Believe it or not, in some instances, healthy eating and pleasure do intersect. The desire for food is a basic need that we all must satisfy on a regular basis. Similarly, we all have an attitude or a point of view around what we experience and encounter daily. Individuals have food preferences. Unique are the ways that we view experiences and how we choose to feel about what we encounter. In satisfying the desire to enjoy a snack, one may

select ice cream, while another may choose fresh fruit, a tasty salad, or popcorn. The selection around a common desire (food) is likely a choice specific to the individual's tastes and preferences. Your attitude is much the same. You choose how you react to the events and people around you.

In this scenario, we have to assume that you choose what you eat. While someone else may select your snack, only you can choose your attitude. In keeping with the food theme, how you choose to react and approach life may be best described as your *appetite* for certain things. You make conscious decisions to feed your positive thoughts and feelings or feed the adverse and negative side of your persona. The choices you make and your orientation to life drive and nourish your attitude. Because life is seldom simple, we constantly face making tough decisions regarding whether we wish to focus on and accentuate positives or negatives. My friend, the simple answer to this complex dilemma lies in your choice of whether you wish to focus on the positive or negative experiences that life presents to you. After all, it is your choice. This is personal! Before the naysayers begin lining up, do not misinterpret the message here. I am not looking to get you to sign up for some pie-in-the-sky, everything-will-always-be-all-right-and-turn-out-well concept. That would be naïve, superficial, and misleading. You would never believe that type of messaging anyhow. Many of the things that happen to us and take place in our lives are beyond our influence and control. What you and I can control is how we choose to react to those situations and events.

Now that the proverbial ice has been broken and we are beyond a few basic concepts related to attitude, I want to spend some time examining the importance of attitude. Why give all the attention to attitude, and what is all the fuss? For starters, your attitude and orientation to life become your metaphorical lens of life. We know there are many amazing individuals in this world who are not able to use their eyes for vision, as the majority of us can. Many of these same individuals are extraordinary visionaries even in the absence of physical sight. The type of vision and sight I am referring to here extends

far beyond the process of your brain translating images through your physical eyes. Your view is your perspective on life. While blind, Helen Keller provided intriguing insight into her approach to life and living. She was well aware of the many challenges presented by a lack of sight. She was aware of the beauty and many positives that life presented. Ray Charles lost his sight at an early age, yet he saw a world clothed in beautiful music. His creative and ingenious interpretations of melodic lines showered in a new era of music. With that said, literal vision is not necessary for one to have a perspective or point of view. As life's scenarios and experiences become a part of your mental databank, your attitude functions much like the mind with visual images. Your attitude processes all that stimulates you and all that you experience. Your attitude informs you of how you feel about those experiences and provides you with a frame of reference as you anticipate future events and situations.

In a computer, the processor is where computation, problem solving, and the application of programmed logic takes place. The processor is the center of the machine's problem-solving capacity. Think of your attitude as your processor that enables you to determine how you choose to react. Are you influenced by activities around you? I would expect your response to be "yes." Does history and your ability to recall things make a difference? Absolutely! Does prejudice, misunderstood feelings, biases, and misinterpreted situations make a difference? Without a doubt! Life does not take place in a vacuum. We do not live in a bubble. In stating the obvious, we are 100% human and own 100% of how we choose to react to experiences, people, and scenarios.

With ownership comes responsibility, which is what makes your attitude such a big deal. Your reactions and responses have the potential to affect many people and situations around you at any given time. Take a second to think about your life and what you encounter daily. All the joys, surprises, stressful moments, anxieties, triumphs, tragedies, feelings of elation, personal achievements, professional successes, and the feelings you get when you help another individual

may affect you at any given time. This brief list falls far short of capturing all that you encounter. You know your life much better than I could ever begin to describe. Remember, you are the owner of your attitude. In each situation described above, you either make an impact or leave an impression, and in some instances, you accomplish both. You form a perspective or point of view in your mind. You take an approach to life from that point forward based on that specific moment or through the culmination of what you experience collectively from many moments.

The fuss has to do with how you move on from what you experience after the event or encounter takes place. Are you a better person as a result of the event? Do you become sad or depressed? Is your life enriched because of the positive light you brought to someone else? Did some life-changing learning take place that altered the path you were on for an extremely long time? Was your perception of an individual or group of individuals forever changed? The fuss is that your attitude in response to these things affects your outlook and in many instances, affects others, either immediately or down the road.

Each of us is uniquely and wonderfully made. Our attitude is a major part of our uniqueness. It sets us apart and sets us on our life course. Your attitude can keep you moving forward in a positive manner or conversely initiate your regression. Your attitude can cause you to stay right where you are mentally or physically, sometimes against your will or better judgment. Anything you do or achieve in life is linked to or driven by your attitude. Think about this powerful statement. Your thoughts, feelings, actions, activities, and orientations to life are affected and driven by your attitude.

In and around the sports world and among sports commentators there is a cliché and catchphrase we often hear when the big game is on the line or when a team is at a critical point in the game. We often hear that a team or an opponent needs to take a *gut check* or examine their intestinal fortitude at that point within the game or match. Of course, the commentators are not describing some elaborate physical exam that needs to take place mid-game. They are describing the

need for the players to engage in a bit of courageous self-inspection to make a big play, hold their ground, or survive to win.

I hope you gained insight from this chapter. I want to conclude it by asking that you engage in what I will call an *Attitudinal Checkup*. What is this Attitudinal Checkup all about, and how do I complete it? I am glad you asked! In a bit of self-inspection, ask yourself a few or all of the questions that follow to determine how you typically respond to people and situations. Remember this is all about your attitude, so be very honest with yourself. No need to keep score; this is a mental checkpoint, and there is neither a passing or failing score.

Attitudinal Checkup I: Significance of Attitude

- Do you tend to look for the positive or the negative in people or situations, and why?
- Do you often feel overwhelmed and powerless, knowing success will be difficult if not impossible?
- If you approach situations with bold confidence, knowing you can achieve success, what drives those feelings?
- Do you learn from important encounters and try to apply knowledge gained to future situations?
- Do you feel a responsibility to improve the lives of others?
- If you seem to float along with a mindset of "whatever happens, happens" does it frustrate you or excite you, and why?"
- How does it make you feel knowing that other people are affected by how you respond to them and that you own your responses 100% each and every time?
- How do you feel regarding your level of *attitudinal stamina* to navigate the complexities that will come your way?
- Describe how you recognize and celebrate small successes along the way in anticipation of greater things to come.
- How does your approach to life, people, and situations

positively align with the things you hold most important to you and support your quest toward achieving positive outcomes throughout your life?

This checkup is essential before we continue our dialogue and will function in concert with other action items forthcoming in this book to set you up for success. This exercise was designed to get you seriously thinking about where your attitude resides and where your starting point may be. Anyone who has traveled and used a map will tell you that an essential part of successful navigation involves knowing your starting point. In the past, before Global Positioning Systems ("GPS"), knowing your starting point was essential. Currently technology no longer requires people to identify where they start; however, when thinking about attitude, identification of where one begins is extremely important. The questions are presented to serve as a guide and help you understand your personal starting point through this journey.

Why did I write this book, you ask? My sincere and simple desire is for you to harness and employ the power of a positive attitude and apply it to improve your life. Your attitude holds amazing power and influence over you. I want you to achieve a world-class positive attitude. I understand that what I am challenging you to do is easier said than done, but I have faith in your ability to do it. You own your attitude and have the responsibility to ensure that you properly nurture it. Once developed, take your positive attitude to a world-class level of positivity. In the next chapter, I will cover in greater detail the impact of ownership and what it should mean to you.

AFFIRMATION #1

I affirm that from this day forward I will take complete responsibility as owner of my attitude.

CHAPTER **2**

Impact: The Small Details and the Big Picture

"Attitude is a little thing that makes a big difference"

—Winston Churchill

Your attitude has a tremendous impact on your life and the lives of others. I hope by now you will at least agree with me that much. There is a great deal of truth to my opening statement. If you need proof, think about your responses to the *Attitudinal Checkup* from chapter one. If you perform a word search or look up the word *impact,* you will find a few meanings. According to Dictionary.Com, here are the two meanings most applicable to this chapter: As a verb, the word means to have an effect on; to influence or alter. As a noun, the meaning conveyed by the word *impact* is influence or effect. Strangely enough, influence is central to the meaning of impact, even when used in different forms. The impact of attitude relates to the influence your attitude has on others and on the situations and scenarios you encounter. There is no escaping this concept. Your attitude has influential power. You own it 100%, all day, every day.

There are myriad factors that may influence why you feel a certain way. While this is true, the attitude you possess and display influences people and situations. Now let's not run off thinking that you hold some mystical power over other people. That clearly is not the case.

What you do have is the ability either to positively or adversely influence others and future events depending on the attitude you choose to display.

In the opening chapter, I established what constitutes your attitude. Now let's go deeper to understand why the fuss as it applies to your attitude. Your existence is neither haphazard nor by chance. My faith tells me that when you were created, an incredible destiny already existed for your life, long before you took your first breath. The fact that you are here by divine destiny means your life inherently has a purpose. You are not just passing through. You are not merely wasting time for a few years waiting for the next great thing to take place. With that said, you have a responsibility to leave a positive mark on the situations and people you encounter. Once again, I am talking about your influence. Your attitude and approach to life become your portal to show the world your positive influence. As stated in the lines above, you own your attitude 100%. If your attitude is poor, it is yours, and the resulting poor influence belongs to you. If you have an attitude of fear, you own it and will likely operate in a manner that produces fearful results. If your approach to life is filled with optimism and a belief that positive outcomes are in your path, you will likely possess a contagious optimism that allows you to have a positive influence on others.

This message is not to say that everything will always turn out fine or that you will not encounter struggles and difficulties. If you are seeking that storyline, my writing will disappoint you. My purpose is to help you understand your attitude and the amazing power of possessing a positive attitude. Understand that I possess neither the foresight nor the power to conjure a happy ending for anyone, including myself. You do not have that power either. What you do have is the power of choice. You ultimately choose how you will react to your stimulus.

Going a bit deeper to understand your attitude means you have to examine how you feel about things, up close and personal. Ideally at this point you are not feeling that you are standing on the sideline or

that you are some casual observer. If you are still reading this book, you have already made a commitment toward improving your understanding of a very important part of who you are. You owe it to yourself to continue. You may ask, what are the small details, and how do they relate to me? I am happy you asked those important questions. The small details are your beliefs, thoughts, feelings, values, spheres of influence, and your environment. As I continue to write, I already hear someone saying, "Those are by no means small details when you consider the magnitude that any single factor may have." Agreed, and when confronted in combination, the impact can be overwhelming. How you deal with these details and the feelings you carry away from your encounters define your attitude, and your attitude can define who you are. Now it is time for another self-inspection exercise. Once again, there is no passing or failing score; the purpose is to get you to think about the details that shape your attitude.

Attitudinal Checkup II: Navigating the Details

- What are your beliefs, and what life factors have served to shape your beliefs throughout your life?
- Are your beliefs easily swayed or influenced by external factors? Describe why or why not.
- If your thoughts were displayed for the entire world to see, would you be proud or ashamed of what the world would see?
- How much does it matter to you what other people think of you?
- Are you quick to form judgment, or do you carefully consider the most important facts when determining how you feel about something or someone?
- Do you often have feelings of regret based on the interaction you have with others or based on the influence you have on situations?

- What are the things in your life that you value the most?
- Who are the individuals who influence you the most, and why?
- Describe the kind of influence you believe you have on those you encounter.
- Based on the reactions of others, what kind of influence are they communicating that you have? (If unclear, you need to ask.)
- Describe the healthy environments where you seek to dwell that are capable of bringing out the best in you.
- Describe your level of your ability to discern when you are operating in an unhealthy environment.
- Describe your level of personal courage to remove yourself from an unhealthy environment when possible.

Reading through this section may not take you very long. Because this is not a race to the finish, take some time for an in-depth self-inspection based on your responses. You may be surprised by your answers and responses. You own your beliefs, thoughts, feelings, and values. You have a great deal of ownership within the spheres of influence and environments where you operate. If you were to think of your life as a large global business organization, you would be the CAO—chief attitude officer. Your responsibility would be to understand and lead yourself in a healthy existence through effective attitude leadership. I am very intentional in using the word *lead* in the context of this sentence. Later I will deal with the concept of leadership as it applies to your attitude, but I wanted to plant the seed now. We can watch your leadership capabilities sprout, take root, and grow through this message with the intent of developing your attitude into a mighty tree in your life, deeply rooted in fertile soil.

The impact of ownership means that your orientation around your beliefs, thoughts, feelings, and values are just that: yours. You own how these factors inform your attitude. Remember, you make

conscious decisions and choices to engage your attitude based on these factors. With ownership comes responsibility. Some forms of ownership carry legal implications. Let's look at the act of purchasing a house. Far beyond merely being a financial transaction, buying a home includes major legal rights and responsibilities for the purchaser and the seller. The same may be stated regarding your attitude. You have the right to form your personal perspective or attitude about anything and everything in your life. No one can deny you of that option. You have a responsibility for the impact and influence you have on others based on the attitude you own and display. In some instances, you carry the burden of either consequences or the joys from the benefits that accompany your attitude, but that fact does not totally take others off the hook. After all, you are one of the data points they will use to determine their perspective and attitude. As it relates to your attitude, what types of data are you providing the world? Are you the highlight of someone's day in a positive way, or are you the plague everyone seeks to avoid at all costs? If you could somehow have an out-of-body experience and observe yourself interacting with others and navigating through life, would you be pleased with what you see, or would you disgust yourself in seeing the same behaviors and negative actions you often criticize others for possessing? Perhaps I should have saved that question for our next Attitudinal Checkup; however, I could not wait that long.

The first section of this chapter addressed you; after all, you are the focal point of this narrative. Because there are more pages ahead for your reading pleasure, the conversation does not end here with you. Let us now examine the bigger picture of why others are important. Each person is here on this earth to make a difference in life. Each person can change situations and impact (there is that word again) people. Each person breathing is an active participant in this journey called life. You may challenge this notion and question how an infant changes situations and influences others. If you understand and have ever witnessed the miracle of human development and childbirth, you probably have a good sense of the level of complexity involved

with an infant entering this world. An infant who survives a challenging developmental path and a difficult delivery while only a few minutes old and yet who remains positive about life can provide a level of optimism and hope for someone feeling hopeless and doubtful.

A great artist or orator can inspire and lift the spirits of others. A well-placed smile or a verbal "thank you" can cause someone to have a wonderful day or a positive experience. An individual with skewed values or beliefs can bring others down and cast a dreaded shadow over situations. Whatever the scenario and regardless of the situation, the common thread lies in the individuals' stories, not as much how they felt, but what placed them in their respective situation and how we feel about those individuals. The story is nothing more than the facts and details—data. Your feelings about the story formulate your attitude. Your attitude has great implication and influence on everyone you encounter from that point in time with your personal experiences onward. What you experience, how you feel about it, and how you think about it affects your impact on others, and that is your big picture.

Take a few seconds to consider all the people you contact and interact with on a regular basis. Consider your chance or non-routine encounters. Think about all of the situations whereby you have an opportunity to make a difference. Consider the times when you wished you could retract something you said or did. Whether in a positive or negative sense, you make a difference. As an agent of positive change, it is crucial to understand and master your ability to make the most of the difference you make through your attitude.

Many years ago, my wife and I were preparing for the arrival of our first child. As first-time parents, we were filled with the joy of our blessing and sought to progress down the road of my wife carrying and delivering our baby. Late one November evening, approximately four months into the pregnancy, we found ourselves rushing to the hospital for immediate relief from the pains and trauma my wife was experiencing. What was happening, and what could go wrong with our perfect miracle? At 3:59 a.m. on December 1, we were faced

with the loss of our child. Needless to say, our healing took time. We often wondered if healing would ever happen. How long would we suffer, and what had we done to deserve this heart-wrenching outcome? Initially there appeared to be nothing positive from the situation. It was one of those times when people could legitimately question their faith and belief. How was I to put all this information and pain together and determine how I felt about what happened? What type of attitude was I going to develop? Certainly it was a tough situation and the greatest loss I had ever faced. I was thankful my wife survived and was still by my side. I did not take that fact for granted. The situation majorly affected my attitude in ways that I had never known up to that point in my life. I had a decision to make. Would I choose to be bitter and resentful, wishing we had never begun the wonderful journey that turned tragic? Would I resign myself to feeling eternally sorry for our loss?

Two things made the difference for me. First was my faith, my prayers, and the prayers of others, which brought me comfort through that dark time. Each gave me strength when I needed it most and helped me maintain my bearing through the loss. The second factor was my attitude and how I chose to deal with the situation. You see, I learned a hard lesson about taking life for granted and that each and every day counts. The pain eventually subsided, and of course, life waits for no one. That experience provided me with the right attitude and mental tenacity to move forward. A few years later we were blessed with the miracle of conception once again and eagerly yet cautiously moved down the path of my wife carrying our unborn child toward delivery. With my reconstructed attitude in tow, I witnessed the miracle of our daughter's birth. With her, I do not take a single day for granted, and I am thankful for her every moment of my life. Every step while preparing for her delivery and every decision regarding her welfare now is born out of the desire to make a positive difference in her life. As she grows, I still need the prayers and my faith in God, although for different reasons now. Additionally, it is my attitude that continues to shape how I approach the awesome

responsibility of parenting. I owned my attitude and the choices that came with it 100%. I owned the benefits and consequences that came with it. **Life can be a tough teacher; however, with the right attitude and tenacity, you can endure the lesson.**

Choose your attitude carefully; others are depending on you to make a positive difference in their lives. Closer to home, a possible source of strength for you may be your attitude and perspective on life. In your moment of darkness, your attitude may get you through. Your perspective and approach to situations may be the support you need at a time when you may not feel you are strong enough to stand on your own. You see, this message is far from being simply a feel-good one. Part of my goal is to present you with useful and usable concepts that have the power to change your life. In our next chapter, we will examine a model that may yield success or failure, all based on your attitude. You own your attitude, along with the benefits or consequences that accompany it, and we will examine how this ownership may play out for you.

Affirmation #2

I affirm that I will maintain a positive attitude while enduring the many challenges and trying situations (and people) that come my way.

CHAPTER 3

The Cycle: Attitude–Thoughts–Actions–Outcomes–Consequences

A positive attitude in life is as essential as breathing.

Many events and occurrences in life happen either by process or as a matter of cycle. Life and nature operate based on a cyclical nature that exists among living organisms. Seasons and accompanying weather patterns change according to a divinely established cycle. Electrical currents may be measured and expressed through cycles. When one examines life in a holistic sense, we tend to compartmentalize specific zones of life into cycles based on age. Attitude is no different and is an essential part of your life cycle. In my previous dialogue, I established what constitutes your attitude and how the small details leave an indelible mark on the big picture. Now it is time to examine a cycle we launch hundreds of thousands of times, if not millions of times, throughout our lives. This is no secret; everyone does it regardless of race, gender, height, weight, language, culture, or any other means of viewing people. Here is my concept, simple yet profound: **Your attitude impacts your thoughts, which impacts your actions, which creates outcomes, which hold consequences.**

This extremely simple model describes what happens to you repeatedly throughout your day, week, over the years, and throughout your life.

The Infinity Attitude Cycle

While still building on the discussion around attitude, this notion calls for us to examine and establish attitude as our starting point to demonstrate the importance of getting this part of the cycle correct. One could prematurely conclude that attitude is the result and sum of all experiences and feelings that cause you to feel a certain way or believe in certain things. If the focus and direction of your life dealt with only you, in the absence of anyone else, you would be on the path to success. After all, in that world, who else or what else matters? You would be in your little utopia or self-created kingdom or queendom. If you are familiar with space travel, you will recall that on returning to the earth's atmosphere, spacecraft experience intense heat upon reentry. As you re-enter reality from your personal utopia, avoid getting burned up in space by coming back at an incorrect trajectory or the wrong velocity, metaphorically speaking, of course. This world and this life were never designed to be solely about any one of us as an individual. The kingdom or queendom of "only me" does not exist. The reason it is important for us to get our attitude correct has everything to do with the impact we were created to make and the influence we are capable of having. Remember your purpose and all the things that will fill your waking hours on earth. Attitude has a great deal to do with all that transpires.

How we feel and our point of view (attitude) leads us directly into a discussion about our thoughts and the path our thoughts set in motion within us. Experiences shape us and provide much for us to consider. We develop certain attitudes around situations and about people or groups of people. Before you realize it, your thoughts and thought patterns begin to emerge. What was your attitude toward the individual who cut you off in busy traffic this morning, and what type of thoughts ran through your mind? What was your attitude the last time you were treated unfairly, simply because of your culture or beliefs, and what types of thoughts were you left to handle? Inanimate objects touch us in a major way. What was your attitude toward your beloved vehicle parked in your driveway last week when it did not start? You found yourself stranded in the rain with a big presentation with your boss scheduled for 7:30 that same morning. What kind of thoughts did you possess? And lastly, what was your attitude when you finally reconnected with a friend with whom you fell out of touch many years before, and what types of thoughts did you develop? There is a direct correlation between our attitude and what we think. We own it, we think it, and we live it.

Thoughts have a very powerful influence on our lives. Confucius stated, "**The more man meditates on good thoughts, the better will be his world and the world at large.**" As written by Mahatma Gandhi, "A man is but the product of his thoughts. What he thinks, he becomes." Your attitude plays an important role in shaping your thoughts. A positive and well-oriented attitude has the ability to create positive and productive thoughts, which can lead you to become someone perceived as good and positive as a result of your thoughts. Conversely, a maladjusted attitude may produce negative or unwholesome thoughts that may manifest in what you become and how others relate to you. At the risk of sounding like an automated recording, in either instance, you own it.

Regularly our thoughts compel us to do something or take action. I would say that the majority of the time what we do or how we engage and interact with others is the direct result of what we have been contemplating. Reality check; I fully acknowledge this is not true 100% of the time. I will place this concept into the proper context. I am referring to situations and scenarios whereby one is neither under extreme duress nor in a life-or-death situation. There is a concept called reaction, which kicks in and places us on an instinctive level as opposed to operating on a cerebral level. Let's return to the roadway example used earlier. When you were cut off on the interstate, you formed your attitude regarding the offending driver and had specific thoughts about the individual. You thought about what happened to you, which played out in your mind many times for the next few miles, if not for the remainder of the morning. You may have been very cerebral with your thoughts after the fact. When you received the promotion on your job because of your demonstrated leadership skills and ability to deliver strong results, you were ready with your mentally rehearsed response when the congratulatory compliments began. Again, you would likely operate on a cerebral level through that situation.

Conversely, when parents look out of the kitchen window and sees their child facing a dangerous situation, the instinct to protect the child takes over and leaves very little time for analysis. In that scenario, it is very unlikely that people think about what is taking place and then ponder their thoughts and feelings before leaping into action. Under most normal situations, we think about where we are and what is taking place. Our thoughts are shaped by our attitude.

In taking action, where are you headed, and are you on the right or wrong course based on your thinking? A wrong path may be predicated on an incorrect attitude.

I asked a question previously, and I want to revisit it to make my point. Have you ever wanted to retract words spoken or undo an action you have taken? Even in the challenging game of golf, some nonprofessional tournaments offer you the ability to purchase the

mulligan package that provides you a *do-over* and the opportunity to correct a mistake. I can hear my die-hard golfers saying "We would never do that" or "A stroke is a stroke, regardless of the outcome." This is much the same rule as found in life. We do not have the ability to undo the majority of what has taken place. This concept is something we strive to teach our child on a regular basis. Even if we are saddled with regret, no amount of apology or expression of remorse can retract misplaced words or deeds. The offended may forgive the offender; however, the event has happened. In these instances, forgiveness is not only good; it is an essential element of life. The late Rev. Dr. Martin Luther King, Jr. stated,

"We must develop and maintain the power to forgive. He who is devoid of the power to forgive is devoid of the power to love. There is some good in the worst of us and some evil in the best of us. When we discover this, we are less prone to hate our enemies."

In the spiritual realm, we continually see the concept of forgiveness and why we should be thankful for grace and mercy. We are forgiven and have not received what we rightfully deserve. Without this divine forgiveness, we are doomed.

Returning to the model, our actions are born out of our thoughts. In many instances, our actions take us down a path. Our actions have the capability of driving change. Through our actions, life for us or life for others may be forever changed.

The change described above as a result of actions produces outcomes. An outcome in a simplistic context is described as the result or the product of some preceding occurrence or action. Outcomes may have a tendency and characteristic of being well-intentioned.

Occasionally an outcome is preplanned. Imagine walking into a favorite restaurant thinking you and two friends were getting together for a casual dinner. All day you look forward to the opportunity to

catch up over a great meal and spend quiet time with a small group of individuals of your choosing. You obliviously ignore that fact that other close friends and family members all have plans for that same evening or that many of them are mysteriously not able to share what they are doing that same evening. You do not even notice a few of the cars in the parking lot that would have been a clear indication of something untold. It all comes crashing down on you in a great way, when you and your two friends are escorted to a section of the restaurant packed with thirty individuals gathered in your honor to celebrate some recent accomplishment in your life. You are celebrated, the food is wonderful, and everyone has an outstanding time. A few hours later and for days you still try to determine how such a grand affair was pulled off right under your nose. In this scenario, you saw a positive outcome. Your guests experienced a positive outcome. The event went very well.

Let us examine another scenario with an opposite outcome. Imagine you have a *career day* in the office one Friday. Your boss and the entire senior leadership team are expecting you to provide a status update on an important project. It is career day in your eyes, since you have been looking for the opportunity to make a lasting impression and demonstrate your capability to deliver results as a capable leader. During the days leading up to the presentation, your efforts and actions are unfocused and random at best. You failed to capture what the project was all about and did not articulate an accurate project status. You became distracted along the way and were not able to take advantage of the provided opportunity to display your master creation. In this scenario, your outcome was the result of your actions. Your lack of preparation was rewarded by your falling flat on your face and creating doubt in the minds of others as to whether you have what it takes to excel in your responsibilities. In this scenario, the outcome (failure) is the result of your actions (lack of proper preparation). Although you did not have a positive outcome, the point is that actions in most cases are intentional and begin with how and what we are thinking about a particular situation or event.

When we do or say something, typically an outcome is produced. Seldom are actions performed in a vacuum with no impact. Our outcomes are the result of the actions we engage in and complete. Notice my focus is the action and the direct energy that is transferred to and manifested in the outcome. Intent is not a necessary factor in this illustration. One may argue his or her intentions all day long. I choose to focus on the outcome as a result of the actions taken. Unless we magically gain the ability to read minds, it can be difficult if not impossible to determine an individual's intent. Others may not likely know your intent, but they must, if they are to understand an action you have taken. What others may likely know is that you are wholly responsible for the action you have taken. Others may think you carry a great deal or all of the responsibility for outcomes as the products of your actions. This cause-and-effect scenario has great power, both on the positive and negative side. Many great outcomes have been born from outstanding actions, which have come from positive thoughts, which were led by a positive attitude regarding a situation. Conversely, a poor attitude may lead to negative thoughts and actions that ultimately result in poor outcomes. I hope by now you can see the connection. I am not attempting to *wow* you with some extremely complex equation. My intent is to help you see the connection between critical stages of our behavior.

The last step in this model is consequences. Every outcome creates a set of consequences for us or those impacted by our actions. There are times when we operate in a realm of the unknown when we have no idea of what the potential consequences may be. Sometimes individuals take what I will call the *Vegas* approach to life and situations. You may ask, "What do you mean by the Vegas approach?" I simply mean to imply that the Vegas approach involves playing the odds or entering into a situation hopeful of a positive outcome,

but not necessarily sure. I understand you may argue that unless we are 100% positive of an outcome, we all take the Vegas approach in everything we do. An opposite approach suggests that well-intentioned consequences are the direct result of well-positioned attitudes, thoughts, actions, and outcomes. A popular statement and marketing tagline states "Whatever happens in Vegas stays in Vegas." This fun-intended statement means to convey that all of your Vegas-based secrets will remain just that, in Vegas and a secret. I offer this point of clarification before Las Vegas residents think I am taking an anti-Vegas stance. I have been to Vegas more than once and had a great time during each visit! My reference to Vegas is meant only to illustrate that playing the odds when it comes to consequences is certainly a route one can choose. The more powerful point I am making is that we have the ability to create positive consequences more often by beginning with the right attitude. We do not need to live on the edge of uncertainty or feel that we are the result of random acts and occurrences. Consequences are real, whether intended or not. Consequences make an impact and typically affect someone, somewhere. It could be you or it could be others. Very little takes place devoid of affecting others or other situations.

Our discussion in this chapter focused on the progression from attitude to consequences. In life, the movement from one to the other does not always take the same amount of time as it took you to read about it here. Sometimes this movement seems instantaneous. Here is a simple thought that may assist you in getting the type of outcomes and consequences you desire. Begin with your desired destination in mind and think about the positive outcomes you envision, and then use that information when forming you attitude about a situation. Here is an example to consider. Imagine that you are leading a large initiative with others depending on you to deliver. Of course, you want it to go well with a positive outcome. Begin your initiative with that same result in mind. Let the desire for positive consequences inform your attitude in the beginning. True to our model, attitude will drive your thoughts, which will feed your actions and outcomes. The

resulting consequences will ultimately be the product of what begins with your attitude.

Attitudinal Checkup III: The Attitude Cycle

- ❖ Describe a situation or interaction with another person whereby you had the ability to engage a proper **attitude** from the onset.
- ❖ Describe a scenario when a positive attitude caused you to have positive **thoughts**. Describe a scenario when a negative or problematic attitude caused you to have negative or problematic thoughts. What was the difference between the two examples?
- ❖ Based on your thoughts, what type of **actions** did you take? Were you proud of your actions, or did you regret what happened?
- ❖ Adversely or positively, what was the **outcome** of your actions?
- ❖ Did you influence others in the way you intended based on what started with your attitude?
- ❖ Were the **consequences** you earned through your actions aligned with who you are, and did you successfully add value to the people and situations you were a part of?

My friend, the model is simplistic yet powerful. All elements are interrelated and impact your life. I hope by now I have been able to convince you of the awesome power in possessing the right attitude. Think about it; you control the equation and related components. Once again, you own the outcome and consequences. In our next chapter, we will go further into understanding what else is under our control.

Affirmation #3

I affirm that I will begin applying the Attitude Model to my life to achieve positive outcomes and beneficial consequences.

CHAPTER 4

What Can I Control?

Whether the list of items I control is lengthy or short, my attitude is always at the top of the list.

There once was a young man who was at a point in his life where he felt he was in a relatively good place. Many of the important things in his life seemed aligned with where he thought he should have been at the time. Life was not perfect, yet he felt his current position and the road ahead looked very positive. His comfortable feeling and disposition caused the young man to take on what may be described as an arrogant view of life; not arrogant in the sense of thinking he was better than other people. He became arrogant in thinking he controlled the fate of his life. How proud he was to state and proclaim the following simple, yet misguided statement, "I am the master of my destiny." The young man's screensaver at his place of employment would flash that same statement whenever his computer became idle for an extended amount of time. On the surface, this point of view or even one that expresses extreme confidence sounds harmless. Let us explore what this statement means.

Clinging to those words, "I am the master of my destiny," and believing in the power of those words conveys that one has ultimate control and orchestrates all that will transpire along his or her path. This goes beyond the power of positive thinking. Positive thinking is a productive

mindset and a level of optimism that can sustain you through difficult times and provide a perspective that lifts your spirits. Positive thinking is a mindset that enables one to see opportunity in adverse situations. There is a difference between positive thinking and the notion that one controls one's own destiny. Do not dismiss the power of positive thinking; however, do not confuse a positive mindset with your ability to control what happens to you along your journey.

What you are about to read next is one of the most important elements within this book. Be sure you get it and lock it into the front of your thought patterns. You will always have limited, if any, ability to control the things that are said or done to you. In many scenarios, you will not have the ability to control why events transpire in the manner they do. Even if desirable events happen, you may have limited control over the timing of their occurrence in many instances. *What you can control is how you choose to react to the people you come in contact with and the various events and situations you experience.* As much as we sometimes would like to, or as much as we deceive ourselves into thinking that we can, we cannot control other individuals. There is no magic wand to wave that would cause others say to us exactly what we wish for them say at the time we want them to say it. Unlike with a Hollywood movie or a Broadway play, we are not the director of our life's production. Later, you will have the oportunity to write your own story. We are not in charge of choreographing every move and encounter. I do not control what happens to me, and you do not control what happens to you. At best, we may have the ability to influence other people, scenarios, and situations. I stress *may*, since that level of influence has no guarantee. As examined using our equation in chapter three, we learned there is a progression from attitude to consequences. Attitude is the first step in that progression. Your attitude is the lens that informs your thoughts.

Now is not the time to feel like a victim. No need to take on a woe-is-me mentality. Use your newfound or refreshed knowledge regarding how to align your thoughts and energy to focus on the items you can control. This moment should be liberating for many individuals.

To have control over others and all situations is not a casual undertaking. For one to have control means that one has responsibility and accountability for all that one has control over. Is that truly what you desire? Are you looking to be held responsible for the words, actions, thoughts, feelings, actions, outcomes, and consequences of other people? Does this sound like a tempting proposition? Do you wish to be responsible and accountable for everyone you may initially desire to control? Do you wish to carry responsibility for every outcome of each situation you encounter? Do you wish to be on the proverbial hook for every scenario you are a part of? Even if you sincerely reply "yes," do you want to be accountable at all times for everything and everyone? We know that is impossible! You can thank me later; I have just saved you a great deal of worry, concern, heartache, headaches, stress, and agony. I have rescued you from the thought that you are always compelled to take action based on what others are or are not doing. In reality, control is never a casual affair. It is not a part-time job or something we pull out of our pocket when we feel like it. Full control is full-on, all the time. No days off and no vacation. That is the same orientation that we must choose to have regarding how we respond to others and the situations that occur around us. We control how we respond and how we choose to react. Do not yield your control or fall prey to the notion that you can control other people.

Time for another self-assessment to examine where you are and what you can learn about yourself regarding control.

Attitudinal Checkup IV: Control

- Describe how you feel when you are not in control of situations.
- How do you feel when you realize that in many situations, the most you can do is respond appropriately to what you experienced?
- Do you believe it is more important for you to control what begins inside you (your attitude) than it is to seek control over items external to you (people, events, situations)? Explain your response.

- ❖ Do you erroneously equate control with the value you contribute to the people and situations you encounter?
- ❖ Do you believe in the power of influence and look for opportunities to influence individuals and outcomes with your attitude? If yes, provide examples of when you made a difference.

This was a short, yet informative assessment this time. The goal is to get you thinking about your new life, one based on controlling your attitude and your response. This is not a posture of weakness. Now that you are free from the burden of responsibility, use all of your excess energy to focus on your attitude. You may have your hands full dealing with your attitude alone in the absence of trying to control everyone or everything else. My faith informs me that my destiny is controlled and directed by a higher power. Think about what guides your destiny. What are you being led by? What type of infinite wisdom guides your steps? In our life path, we encounter countless situations, and what we control is our reaction to those situations.

By now you may wonder what happened to the young man obsessed and deceived into thinking that he controlled his destiny. What a poor guy. How could anyone be that mistaken? Do not feel too sorry for him. After a few of life's lessons caught up with him, he learned the proper orientation and approach to his destiny and what he was able to control. Once I learned that important lesson, I was able to move forward with much greater ability to focus on the people and items I could influence. I was only fooling myself. Thankfully, before I spent too much time in that dream world, I came back to consciousness. I learned that control is not synonymous with impact.

In the next chapter, we will focus on the role that your power of choice plays in understanding your attitude.

Affirmation #4

I affirm that I will no longer worry about or become frustrated by situations I cannot control.

CHAPTER 5

Your Choices

Both a positive attitude and a common cold are contagious. Given a choice, which would you rather have?

Life conditions people to think in terms of limits and constraints placed on their life, or they think about the seemingly endless limits within the world where they live. At an early age, we learned behaviors based on what our parents or guardians permitted us to do. Our childhood landscape was riddled with rules of the road, most often set by those responsible for our well-being and entrusted with our care. At the same time, a certain childlike curiosity and innocence drove our ability to dream about the future with a boundless domain. We learned how far to stray from our parents' line of sight before we heard their voices or saw their eyes searching for us. We knew how to dream the most fabulous tales of what we wanted to be when we grew up without many limits placed around on we believed was possible. No one had to lecture us about the many dangers of becoming a firefighter. No one had to paint a picture for us to visualize the joy of becoming a famous singer or musician. While young, whatever you dreamed of becoming, you were almost there in thought alone. As we grow older, life has a way of reducing our limits and possibilities compared to when we were younger. Life began imposing more constraints on many individuals. For others, the process of maturing

opened up a new realm of possibilities for them to pursue.

In either a constraint-filled scenario or one filled with boundless limits, there are choices that individuals must make. Many factors play a role in determining whether boundaries keep you within a defined space or whether you dream without limits. Though you may feel as though you are continuously a victim of life or subject to circumstances swirling around you, personal choices are made on a regular basis. You may or may not choose with whom you interact. You may not choose how you are affected by various events and happenings around you. In some instances, even when you have the liberty of choice, you may not choose the timing of the interaction or when a situation may occur. The ability to choose "the what" and "the how" could easily resemble the ability to exercise control over others and events. Since we resolved our desire to control other people and situations in chapter four, we no longer have control issues. Should any of those urgings persist, feel free to reread chapter four at any time. If you are doing your victory dance because you are totally over thoughts of control, let us continue moving forward.

Regardless of whether our interactions with others are positive or painful or whether we feel like we are a victim or victor, one fact remains constant. Each of us has the power to choose how we react to other people and situations. Factors may influence the choices we make. Our values and beliefs play a role in our choices. Each person's experiences play a role in their choices. The same thought process is equally applicable to the attitude we possess about people and situations. We choose the attitude that we carry into conversations in many instances. We own our attitude and our resulting thoughts that we develop along the way from our interactions.

Choices are powerful and may yield long-lasting and life-changing results. Think for a few minutes about some of the most important decisions you have made over your lifespan. How might those choices have been different had your attitude, which guided those choices, been different? There may be adults who now realize that a different attitude toward homework and school could have led to the

development of a level of mental tenacity and stamina necessary to do well in their studies. In doing well as opposed to barely making it, their opportunities as adults would be significantly different. In this instance, a positive change in attitude toward school as a young person can eliminate barriers and limitations later in life. You may say that this concept is entirely too simple; life is much more complex than what you are proposing. I agree with you totally; life is complex, and we have quite a lot to handle. I never said life was easy. Given the alternative, I choose to make the most of the life I have been blessed to have. A positive aspect required to make the most of it involves my approach to life, which directly involves my attitude. Choice of attitude makes a difference! How we react makes a difference! Allowing your attitude to become informed by accurate and positive information plays as large of a role as having your attitude informed by negative and erroneous information.

By now you probably already recognize the familiar format below and know what is next. If you guessed another Attitudinal Checkup, you are correct. Now sit up and prepare to think introspectively once again.

Attitudinal Checkup V: Choices

- ❖ How do you feel about your ability to choose the way you interact with others and the attitude you display as the result of those interactions?
- ❖ In thinking about choosing your attitude, are you able to make the connection between thoughts, actions, outcomes, and consequences? How do you feel about the relationships among them?
- ❖ Do you feel that choosing your attitude and orientation toward people and life's events makes you more accountable for your outcomes and consequences? Explain how this works for you.
- ❖ If you chose an inappropriate attitude relative to another person or situation, what did you learn from that experience that may prove essential to you going forward?

No need to respond out loud; the goal is for you to apply some mental muscle toward thinking about the type of attitude you chose to possess and the resulting consequences that accompany your attitude toward people, events, and situations.

As I pointed out early in our discussion, life has not always provided me with favorable situations, and I am sure there are countless other people with myriad scenarios that may make my experiences pale by comparison. Regardless of what any of us encounter, we have the common ability to choose our attitude or reaction to whatever occurs. Because of our uniqueness, we typically make different choices. My point is that you have the ability to shape your attitude in spite of what you are confronted with. I urge you to believe in the power of the choices you make that shape your attitude. If this is new territory for you, pray and ask for guidance. In training your mind and conditioning your attitude, you will begin to consciously gravitate toward the outcomes and consequences you desire as opposed to forever feeling a hopeless victim of circumstances.

I have a story to share with you to demonstrate the power of making the right choice with respect to your attitude. When I caught up with a close friend over lunch, he shared the following account regarding a situation he faced and his reaction. More important than the events that took place were the choices my friend made throughout the encounter. To conceal the identity of my friend and protect the confidentiality of the situation, I will refer to him as James.

James was employed by a large company and was extremely confident in the quality of his results and felt great about his standing with the company. James had been employed by the firm for several years and had a stellar record, unblemished by any incidents or behaviors deemed problematic to the firm. By all indication, James was well on his way toward building a remarkable track record with his employer. He was a consistently strong performer with a bright future ahead of him. James was excited about his future and thought that his chance to move ahead was just around the corner. One morning James was called in to speak with his boss and another member of the leadership

team. Thinking the conversation could hold only great news, James entered the room rather enthusiastically and welcomed the opportunity for the meeting. James was greeted professionally, and he settled into his chair for what he expected to be a great conversation.

As the conversation began, James heard words that were previously unthinkable. His boss informed James that the firm was going to release him immediately because of information that was returned from law enforcement officials revealing a criminal act on his record committed many years in the past. James, while fully understanding the seriousness of the meeting, initially thought that the managers were trying to pull a "fast one" on him before getting to the real reason for the meeting. James soon realized that the conversation was not a joke and they were serious in their intent to escort him out of the building at the conclusion of the meeting. James was not unfamiliar with the untimely news of associates being released because of downsizing or right-sizing. Such occurrences often happen without notice or warning. James witnessed such an occurrence of it happening in the past to another member of the team. The delivery of that type of news had become commonplace in the industry where James was employed. Additionally, James knew that his record was clean. He had no criminal activity ever, no reason for anyone to conclude that he had a troubled past, and certainly not one that would threaten his ability to maintain employment with any company. When I tell you that his record was clean, there was not even a jay-walking infraction or speeding ticket present. On the inside, James knew he was of great character and unshakable integrity. Something erroneous must have occurred.

As the conversation unfolded, James learned that he would have a few minutes to gather his personal items and place them in a box in preparation for the unscheduled journey home. Still, he could not believe what was happening to him. Someone somewhere had made a gross mistake. How and why would the firm have hired him with such a major infraction on his record? How was this erroneous information unfairly linked to him, and what could he do to resolve

the misunderstanding? These and many other questions ran through James's head. One of the final requests that James had was to make a phone call to the Human Resources Team to straighten out the misunderstanding and clear up the situation. His request was denied, and the team was unwilling to discuss the situation any further.

Many thoughts circled in James's mind. The entire event caught him unprepared for any well-thought-out or prepared response to what was taking place. In the span of a few minutes, James's perspective of his position with the firm went from being a proven performer and leader to that of an outsider. What was going on, and why was it happening? As the meeting concluded, James stood and faced the managers and graciously thanked them for their time and expressed his appreciation for the opportunities afforded him as a member of the team. James did what would be difficult for many others in the same situation. He was thanking and showing appreciation to the individuals who were about to walk him out of the door and toss him out on the street.

James went back to his desk and packed personal items. He then called his wife, who happened to work from home that day, to ask her to pick him up. She could not believe the news, and they both tried to make sense out of what was extremely senseless. Once home, James did what he wanted to do in the presence of his managers. He called Human Resources to get more information and discuss his termination further. Once James was able to speak to the representative, the call began like any other call to HR would. Soon after all of the proper verification was completed, it became painfully aware to James that the voice on the other end of the phone had some level of familiarity with his termination and potentially the reason for the call. James and his family were deeply rooted in their faith and had already asked for divine guidance through his trial. James, though cloaked with disbelief in what was taking place, already had a sense of calm about him as the conversation progressed.

James questioned what was found on his record and the nature of his dismissal from the firm. The personnel representative shared with

him as much information as legally possible regarding the specifics. James imparted the same line of reasoning that raced through his head since the moment he was first made aware of the reason for the decision to release him. A mistake had been made somewhere by someone, he insisted. The personnel representative understood his assertion and proceeded to log notes into the system to document the details of the conversation. Within the conversation, James received important information that stood out like a fire truck blaring down an otherwise quiet street at 3:30 a.m. Based on the date of the conviction on his record, James would have been approximately seven years old at the time of the offense. Clearly James was in no position to have committed an illegal offense anywhere close to what was on his record at that age. The representative continued the discussion with James and proceeded to verify once again information to ensure that all the facts were correct. James was able to communicate with the director of HR to make his case. Through this process, the conversation changed when the analysis revealed that the offense in question was tied to James in error by way of an identically named individual who recently sought employment in the same firm. The director clearly saw the reason for the mix-up and the error of the decision to terminate James.

James continued the conversation, and by the time the discussion concluded, he had his job back and was welcomed to return to the site the following day to resume his employment. James remained confident and optimistic through the entire exhausting day and happily returned to the office the next day. Only a few fellow teammates were nearby when he was released; thus, his departure and return the next day were unnoticed by the majority of the employees. James met with his manager and the same members of the leadership team that greeted him a day earlier with the unsettling news. They offered profuse apologies as well as the explanation that the action taken was required by Human Resources and company procedures based on the adverse nature of the discovery. James understood and expressed that he knew all along that somehow a mistake had been made. The

team concurred that they had been nothing less than impressed with the level of professionalism and superior results that James had always produced. They viewed James as a leader and looked forward to his continued contributions. James concluded the meeting with the managers and returned to his desk to resume his career with the firm.

James's world was turned upside down for roughly twenty-four hours. He heard the unthinkable and experienced firsthand undeserved consequences of someone else's mistake. Through his horrific scenario, James made choices along the way regarding his attitude and how he would react to what was happening to him. Think about what you now know about James's situation. James made choices that positioned him to maintain a healthy and forward-thinking attitude through his personal crisis. James understood the big picture of what was taking place and why it was important to keep his head *in the game* as opposed to displaying a negative reaction at the moment. James's attitude informed his thoughts and actions. James understood and reacted to the cause of his situation, the erroneous information. He chose not to focus on the individuals who delivered the news. James's actions were based on what he could control and did not allow emotion or reaction to events outside of his control to derail his efforts to resolve the situation.

Although James's situation is unique, think about the many opportunities you have on a daily basis to choose your attitude based on what you experience and what is happening around you. The opportunity to claim *victim status* and begin a downward spiral of victim mentality plagues far too many individuals. Ask yourself this: How many times do you find a victim in the winner's circle? Flying into a rampage in the face of adversity would have done little to advance James's quest for justice and resolution. How much does the same reaction advance your cause within the scenarios that come up in your life? Let me be very clear; certain situations evoke instinctive reactions with no time for an attitudinal inspection. Thankfully we are wired with a fight-or-flight mechanism for our safety. Those are not the situations I am referencing. James was in neither a life-or-death

nor fight-or-flight situation.

You can relax momentarily before moving on to our next chapter. There is no Attitudinal Checkup waiting for you at this point. Your number-one task to master is to understand and apply the power of the choices you make about your attitude. James made great choices that set him up to resume his career without question. In fact, James exhibited a great deal about his core character as the direct result of the choices he made in his situation. I can imagine that there are many who would say to me, "Kenneth, this was an easy one. A simple review of the facts would have resolved this one exactly as it happened." Yes, I understand that point of view. Either a deeper inquiry performed by Human Resources or a legal reversal may have ensued and clarified the mistake. What James would not have been able to reverse or retract is the perception he created in the minds of others as the result of his attitude getting the best of him in his situation. Regardless of how profuse the apology, words said cannot suddenly become unsaid and things done cannot become undone. Your choices, especially as they apply to your attitude, matter. Choose wisely and develop the skill of choosing well. Develop the discipline of making beneficial and well-informed choices. In the next chapter, I will spend some time discussing what to remember and what to forget, so join me.

Affirmation #5

I affirm that I will intentionally make good choices that will fuel my positive attitude and my perspectives toward life.

CHAPTER 6

Foster Learning while Developing Selective Amnesia

Do not allow a negative attitude to become your kryptonite.

Previously the discussion centered on choice and understanding the power that choice has while informing our attitude. In an ideal world, one would find ample time to consider all known factors to make the best choice each time. How great life would be if immediately after a conversation or interaction, you had the ability to press the *pause* button to assess your attitude, formulate your response, and choose your actions. Many faulty or misguided responses could have been avoided. Many missed opportunities could have been taken advantage of, if only you had a few minutes or seconds to consider the merits or pitfalls before choosing your attitude. In some instances, you may have the ability to defer response or postpone comments and reactions. As parents, one of the truths we toil to impart to our daughter is that *not every comment, situation, or event requires an immediate response, and some do not merit a response at all.* On the surface, the lesson could be perceived as one with the intention of producing a less-talkative child in selected moments. The lesson we seek to teach is not about quantity or frequency of words. The learning is about helping her take the time, when available, to think

about her attitude and reaction before providing an immediate or thoughtless response. Life teaches us that we do not always have time to walk away from people or situations to develop a well-thought-out response. Visual clues indicative of our attitude may be immediately on display long before the first word is ever spoken.

One may surmise that this expectation is a large one to place on a child, when many adults are not able to demonstrate such a level of discipline. I will reason that a greater number of us would be in a better place now, had we learned this lesson or learned it to a greater extent earlier in life. The point I strive to impress is that when you can choose the most appropriate attitude and response, you establish a foundation to support more positive outcomes and consequences. Notice I did not say *perfect* outcomes and consequences. Our goal is to develop a greater number of positive outcomes and consequences. Perfection for most is likely unreasonable and unachievable. Why set yourself up for disappointment?

Experience has shown there are times when an immediate response may be required. In those situations, we most often do what we have trained ourselves to do, and our mind positions us to take on an attitude or response familiar to us. In thinking about your attitude, ask yourself, *how am I consistently training myself to react*? What experiences are you permitting to inform your attitude, such that new reactions fall into the same patterns both positively and negatively? How many times do you encounter someone consistently bitter or pessimistic because of countless patterns of doubt ingrained in that individual? Adverse thoughts may become so deeply ingrained that the individual's core attitude is always one of doubt and pessimism. On the other side of the coin, have you ever encountered an individual who consistently approaches others and situations with an open perspective, ready to hear facts and information before forming judgment or reacting? What about the individuals who consistently look for positive elements or take ownership for their personal success regardless of what is going on around them? In each scenario, individuals make a conscious choice of the attitude they take into situations and interactions.

Let me say that you are not reading the same material twice. Well, not exactly, I wanted to take a moment to review and establish the foundation for this chapter. Much of when we react and how we react is based on our personal history and experience. Our attitude, thoughts, and feelings are in many instances informed by our same history and experience. Your mind is the greatest repository of information regarding your perspectives, fears, joys, apprehensions, desires, ambitions, concerns, triumphs, and tragedies. For some individuals, there may not be much to manage. For others, keeping up with all of these data points and informational nuggets is quite a challenge. Some do an excellent job of focusing solely on thoughts, experiences, and important events. These individuals do not forget everything else. They just choose not to focus on the items that are comparatively less important. For my techies out there, imagine a primary app running with other apps operating in the background. They may be important to the overall function yet not primary at the moment. Others may feel as though the perfect metaphor of their life is that of a leaf blowing in the wind. Every single current that comes along may seem to toss them about and send them flailing in the winds of life. You know where you are much better than I do, and I am not here to judge based on where you are.

What I do propose is that you either develop or advance your methods of learning selective amnesia. This advice may sound contradictory, and in a sense it is. I will state this challenging concept in the most simplistic terms that come to mind. Certain situations, events, experiences, thoughts, and reactions need to be forgotten. Quite frankly, some of the *baggage* individuals choose to carry adds no value. Some information should be carried forward and placed to your permanent memory as guiding principles for future events on your horizon. This information sounds easy on the surface: keep the gold and throw out the junk. Your task is to become the master gatekeeper in deciding what to keep and what to discard. Additionally, it would be wise to master when to discard certain information files. Stay with me; I did not say that this task was easy. Let's go a bit deeper.

Here is the challenge within the challenge: You must learn from the golden moments as well as learn from the junkyard moments in your life. You see, this is real talk for real people. I am not attempting to lead you down a path of flowers and total joy, thinking that everything is 100% great and that you will not have challenges. Life will certainly throw curves your way, sometimes on a regular basis. You know the clichés all too well; "When it rains it pours," "up a creek without paddle," "You can't win for losing," "Crap happens" (yes, I am keeping it clean), and countless more. You probably recognize the many clichés that accompany good times and experiences. "I felt like I soared above the clouds," "I knocked it out of the park," "I was on top of my game."

What you learn, what you remember, and what you intentionally choose not to indulge mentally informs and affects your attitude. **Your memory has the potential to make you or break you.** The ability to apply learning from previous events and situations will make a difference in your attitude. Think back to our model, attitude—thoughts—actions—outcomes—consequences. Within your frame of reference, your self-learning curve is priceless.

Here are a few important factors to keep in mind. Your learning may be reflective or it may be at the moment. Sometimes the "ah-ha" moment happens a week, month, or years later. At the same time, learning can be powerful and immediate. We cannot always predict or anticipate when a learning moment is about to be delivered. Your challenge is to make sure you get the lesson. Be intentional about it. If you do not grasp the lesson, ask yourself, "What is the lesson to be learned or what learning can I derive from the scenario taking place?" Challenge yourself to understand on a higher level what you are going through, the challenges you meet, and the successes you encounter. Without this level of focus, how will you ever know what attitudinal patterns to avoid or replicate? How will you know the best way to navigate future attitudinal pitfalls or how to reap the benefits of engaging the appropriate attitude?

The value in learning the right balance between keeping the gold

and trashing the junk is to use this information to inform your current and future attitude. Quickly turn to the words on this book cover you are holding or at the beginning of my writing on your e-reader. ***Defined by Attitude*** is what you saw, and the important link from this chapter is how you will use this learning to provide an attitudinal definition of who you are.

Your attitude is a dynamic aspect of who you are and how you approach life. Think of the ways you can provide high-quality input that informs your attitude. Think of ways you will need to filter out unwanted and undesirable input that may adversely inform your attitude. Challenge your mind to think regarding capacity and energy. From a capacity perspective, we have already covered the fact that the human mind is capable of receiving, processing, and responding to a great number of inputs and stimuli. I often tell my daughter that the greatest computer she will ever encounter is the one between her ears. Though mental storage capacity is vast, how well are you able to focus on an extremely high number of items concurrently with high-quality effectiveness? I am not referring to one's ability to recall items; I am referring to one's ability to engage at a high level with a large number of thoughts and experiences. Capacity will eventually become an issue for most of us, which is one of the primary benefits of deriving learning and beneficial knowledge from situations along with selective amnesia to leave behind items of input with minimal or no value. It is imperative for each of us to maintain a healthy capacity for continuous learning. Imagine what would happen if your effective storage capacity were filled with only 25% of useful information and the remainder were filled with junk. Adding new information may become problematic, and imagine the task of sifting through all the junk to get to the relevant portion of the useful data and information. Quite an onerous task for sure!

I do not recall where I first heard the following statement: "When you learn some lessons, you must then 'unlearn' them to get what you should have learned the first time." This notion is at the core of learning and selective amnesia. Unlearning may involve breaking adverse

habits and removing yourself from consistently poor ways of thinking. Neither is an easy thing to do. Here are a few questions to inform your forward progress.

Attitudinal Checkup VI: Learning and Amnesia

- ❖ How do you keep track of thoughts and feelings that serve as a mechanism for positive learning that you wish to replicate?
- ❖ Do you require visual reminders of what to avoid and where to place your focus? If you answered yes, what tools will you begin using?
- ❖ Do you enter challenging situations intentionally looking to learn from the experience? If so, how do you capture what you wish to remember?
- ❖ Since most situations in life are not all-or-nothing scenarios, what is your method to harvest the gold while either leaving or learning from the junk (without carrying it with you)?
- ❖ Some of life's lessons are clear and painfully obvious. How well do you rate your ability to understand the cause of what you are experiencing? Think about how you can improve this ability. What will you do differently going forward?
- ❖ What is your mechanism to avoid dwelling within less-than-ideal experiences and outcomes?

The answers to these questions should provide you with the insight of how to leave some thoughts, feelings, and actions in your collective past. Since all is not waste, ideally you are now better armed only to carry with you the gold.

Affirmation #6

I affirm that I will learn from my experiences and release any negatives from my past that adversely influence my attitude and my future.

CHAPTER 7

Attitude = Power to Change Your Approach to Life

If a positive attitude is your lens for life, you will pass the eye test.

As we begin chapter seven, I will take a moment to congratulate you for sticking with our narrative. You have been asked to consider quite a great deal up to this point. We will take a brief moment to celebrate our progress. Three, two, one. Now, let's get back to the task at hand.

There are many metaphors available to make references about one's attitude. In this dialogue, I will spare you all of the farming, agricultural, and water-specific references. I will use the human body to illustrate my point. Think of the attitude an individual has as a muscle or an entire system of muscles. If you were to look at an otherwise healthy, yet less-than-muscular person, you might reason that there are great differences between that person in comparison to an extremely well-cut and defined body builder. While the first may barely exhibit any muscularity, he or she may be perfectly healthy and in premium shape. The second individual may display broad shoulders, sculptured abs, and bulging biceps. The reality is that while body builders may show more muscle mass, they have the same muscles as an individual who may be half their size. So, what is the difference,

you may ask. Typically, the difference is found in how one regularly trains, the amount of resistance encountered on a regular basis (often disguised as exercise) or the intensity of regular exertion. When given proper motion in a safe manner, muscles tend to react in a favorable way. Proper resistance and aerobic challenges create a force that muscles work to overcome and work through. In some instances, overworked and fatigued muscles become sore or may lead to injury. A cycle for positive muscle growth involves a warmup, exertion, cool-down, and then sufficient rest. I will spend more time later in this chapter discussing the importance of what we feed our muscles, so stay with me.

Your attitude functions much like a muscle or group of muscles. Life happens around us every waking second of the day. Your attitude is constantly forced into cycles of warming up, exertion, cooling off, and rest, depending on what you experience at any given time. Some circumstances have a way of immediately thrusting us into the fire without much warmup. Let's face it; unlike going to the gym or taking a long walk, some situations do not always allow you to properly stretch and get the blood flowing for the task ahead. We live and experience feelings and emotions real time, which has an impact on our attitude. From those experiences, resistance, and challenges, we may develop what some people call muscle memory. This term or cliché is used to describe how one's muscles become acclimated to performing in the same way through repetitive motion. Our attitude can perform in much the same manner, and muscle memory can be either helpful or hurtful.

If your attitude is conditioned through repetitive action to embrace change with an optimistic demeanor, you and those around you are the positive beneficiaries of your positive reaction and outlook. Conversely, if situations and experiences have conditioned your attitude to have a troubled reaction to certain experiences you encounter, an adverse type of attitudinal memory comes into play.

Joe is an individual who intentionally looks for positive aspects in his life experiences. Joe is a realist who understands that not

everything will be to his liking or go his way. Joe has a personal statement that he repeats every morning while looking in the mirror. He says aloud,

"This day, I will look to leave as many people as possible in a better state of mind after they interact with me!"

Joe believes in this statement and looks for opportunities to live what he says aloud. One thing that I like about Joe's approach is that it is not unrealistic. Joe does not set himself up for failure by stating that he will leave everyone in a better place. He knows that such a goal is unrealistic and beyond his control. The element of this short story to remember is the value of making a conscious effort to improve situations leave others in a better place as a result of interacting with you. Wow, we need more individuals like Joe in the world, and he is certainly not your "Average Joe." I couldn't resist. Are you able to fathom what life would be like if the majority of the people you know and spend time with were on a personal mission to approach people and situations determined to leave a positive mark as the direct result of their presence and engagement? A very powerful challenge.

Your attitude has amazing power. Your attitude as your portal to the world fuels your ability to change your approach to life. How powerful is that fact, when you consider all you encounter and have to navigate daily? Your attitude becomes the bridge to transport you from where you may currently reside today to a destination of positive relationships with others and a way to keep people and situations beyond your control from tainting who you authentically are. Notice I did not say your attitude will enable you to change the world. You can believe your attitude will change your world. Think about what you can control. Your attitude has the power to affect your approach to the world's challenges and situations.

Before we go much further, it is time to complete another self-assessment or progress check.

Attitudinal Checkup VII: Understanding Your Training Regimen

- How do you plan to consistently approach life's challenges in a manner that allows you to emerge with a perspective that is more positive than negative?
- Similar to Joe's morning routine, what are some of the intentional queues that you could begin giving yourself to facilitate positive attitudinal growth?
- Are you allowing your attitude sufficient rest from life's challenges for recuperation and decompression? If so, do you engage in these rest periods frequently enough?
- What are some of the challenges that may prevent you from keeping a healthy-attitude-building routine?
- How do you recognize repetitive experiences that are not healthy for your attitude, which may require you to remove yourself from the situation, if possible?
- How do you recognize success moments when your attitude positions you to get the most out of an interaction or situation in such a way that you can intentionally seek to have a repeat performance later?

As with previous assessments, my goal is to help you begin or continue thinking of ways to build up your attitudinal muscles in a healthy manner by focusing on an important factor under your control, YOU!

I promised to get back to the notion of feeding your attitude properly. As with physical food, we can ingest junk or we can consume healthy foods. When it comes to our attitude, the methodology is the same. We can exist on a diet of junk that feeds our attitude in a negative way that does not help us in the long run or we can do our very best to engage in a healthy mindset and approach life with a positive approach to building an energy reserve for the long haul. Indeed, life is a marathon, and we have to train appropriately. Our mental diet

and how we train our attitude plays a large role in preparing each of us to become a champion! Ask yourself, "Am I on a junk food diet, or am I engaging in a healthy manner when it comes to my attitude?"

Most health enthusiasts have multiple ways to determine whether they are making acceptable progress toward their goals. Some rely strictly on the bathroom scale, some pay attention to body mass index (BMI) charts, while some use a simple eye test by looking into the mirror with an honest and discerning eye. My point is that you must have a reliable and accurate mechanism or system to determine whether you are making acceptable progress toward your attitudinal goals. How will you know if and when you are making acceptable progress? How will you know when you are ahead of pace or behind? Just as one may see a few extra pounds as the result of a few too many brownies, how will you gauge when you have a few too many adverse engagements to the extent that your attitude begins to knock you off course from being the person you desire to be? You need a system. Others may offer suggestions; however, you must determine what is best for you to get the feedback and information you need to let you know where you are. Perhaps there is a trusted individual you can rely on to offer you verbal feedback. Maybe you begin keeping a simple log of the top three important situations and experiences you encounter during a given day. You can make notes about what the situation was, how you initially felt, what your reaction or response was, and how you felt about the situation once it was over. This log requires intentional effort. While three items per day may not sound like a big deal, doing this the right way is a big deal. Employ the discipline to apply this concept to three items each day. After seven days, take out your notes and think about what you collected while it was still fresh. I am willing to guess that you will begin to see themes emerge from your data. Ideally you will see themes you wish to repeat as often as possible. You will likely observe themes you wish to avoid at all costs going forward. The hook becomes how you should begin thinking about your attitude when approaching people and situations before you are thrown into another fire. You can begin

to anticipate your reaction to certain people and situations in a more thoughtful manner and in some instances with a more consistent approach. Once you employ the level of discipline to do this, you truly can begin to manage your approach to life.

Analogous to being on a healthy living and healthy eating plan, developing a healthy attitude is not easy. You will quickly need to define your level of commitment and in some instances your level of faith and belief in the fact that you can do what it takes to make a difference. If and when you are ready to commit to asking yourself some tough questions and challenging yourself to change your attitude as a means to changing your approach to the world, you will be on the right path.

Your attitude has the power to change your approach to the world by becoming your personal gatekeeper. Your attitude can control your eye gate, your ear gate, and your mouth gate. Your eye gate refers to how you see others and situations at hand. Are you one who looks for the positive or one who seeks every negative aspect about everything around you at any given moment? When it comes to your ear gate, do you only hear, or are you listening to understand what is going on around you? Does your attitude have you spend the entire time during your polite pause thinking only about your verbal retort?

This point in our discussion is a perfect time to transition and make a few observations regarding the mouth gate. When it is your time to respond verbally, have your intentional thoughts regarding attitude prepared you to have an appropriate response? Trust me when I say this and highlight this in your book or on your electronic reader: **words matter!** You can apologize until you turn colors; however, you cannot take back what you have said. In the world of cyberspace, you cannot retrieve errant texts, tweets, e-mails, or instant messages. While it may appear that we have deleted the file or the evidence, in most instances the communication is still out there, and the damage may have already transpired.

I ask that you engage in habit-forming exercises that enable you to assemble positive data points to aid you in achieving a healthy

attitude toward your life and all that you encounter. After all, that is one of the primary reasons you are seven chapters into this dialogue, correct?

In the following chapter, we will take out our scalpel and dissect the word *attitude* for deeper meaning.

Affirmation #7

I affirm that I will regularly engage in a regimen of positive attitude-building exercises in order to achieve a more productive life.

CHAPTER **8**

A.T.T.I.T.U.D.E: What Does It Mean?

Make a positive attitude a part of your success DNA.

My desire is to enlighten you and take you on a journey to understanding your attitude better. I want to show you how to leverage your attitude to experience life with a consistently positive approach. I want you to realize the power of positivity. By now you already know that this is challenging. In this chapter, I will present A.T.T.I.T.U.D.E. as an acronym for deeper meaning and hope it will provide a lighter side of this weighty topic. Before you begin to think this is time off, we are still on task.

I trust it is safe to say you are not tired of hearing about attitude and all that comes along with it. That is great, especially since I am about to add to the list of essential points I want to resonate with you. A few years ago, I had an opportunity to serve as a keynote speaker addressing a room full of young leaders and mentors on a topic near and dear to me. You guessed it; I discussed the virtues and benefits of a positive attitude, as well as a few consequences of owning less than a positive attitude. It was fun then, and little did I know that my approach would serve as the foundation for a chapter within this book. Here we go.

A.

I will begin with the letter **A** representing the word *attitude* in the context that attitude is all about how you affect the people and situations around you. Do you enter the scenario with a sour or defeatist attitude, or do you enter ready to set the world on fire while making a positive impact? For you see, your attitude makes all of the difference between these two extremes and with every point in between. Other people will come to know you by the type of attitude you consistently exhibit before you speak a single word or offer your trademark facial expression. Each act, expression, or word spoken by each of us creates a data point that others may use to judge each of us either favorably of unfavorably. Ask yourself, "What type of proof points am I creating on a consistent basis?"

Do you know someone who is a joy to speak with or with whom you always look forward to interacting? Are there certain situations that always leave you in a good place? Are there others you would avoid if possible, or if you must come in contact with them, it is never a positive experience? Do some situations always seem to get you off your game? The difference may not always lie in the person you encounter or in the type of situation you encounter. In many instances, the difference in how you feel is within and is largely based on your attitude.

T.

The second letter, T, represents *trust*. In many instances, the right attitude is what builds trust between people. Yes, I know this is not an absolute. I will go further. A totally proper and positive attitude cannot preserve trust within a relationship when someone proves untrustworthy, but individuals are more likely to trust another person who is positive and forward-thinking, as opposed to one with a consistently cynical and negative outlook on life. Some levels of cynicism and skepticism add value in certain situations. Most individuals learn to question situations appropriately and often develop a natural instinct that informs them when to move forward cautiously or when not to

proceed at all. Living without such a mechanism would continuously subject each of us to unnecessary risks.

When it comes to building trust, we typically enjoy and move forward in situations with people who have more of a positive demeanor and a can-do attitude. If you think about advertisements, we know that people in marketing have known this fact for years. Within a few seconds, the goal is to get a positive and uplifting individual in front of you to speak about a product or service being offered. If you are watching a longer infomercial-type advertisement, advertisers are counting on you watching while they prove their case. In many instances, negative messages conveyed by a pessimist does not make a positive impact on your attitude. The result is that this type of interaction often does not create trust. Are you likely to trust individuals who consistently convey a poor attitude? Do you believe that others will view you as trustworthy if you consistently display a negative attitude? Unless it is your occupation to bring negative news, and yes, there are such occupations, do you feel that others will go out on a limb to trust you if your consistent persona is negative? One last question before moving to the next letter. If people are consistently negative, how can they expect others to invest positive trust in them?

T.

Trust from the previous section is a direct link to our second T, which represents *tolerance*. Volumes have been written on tolerance for others and how to tolerate less-than-ideal situations. Our attitude plays a major role in how much we can take from situations and other people. With a greater tolerance of you based on the attitude that you display, other people are more willing to build positive relationships with you. These same individuals are likely more willing to remain positively engaged with you. There is a direct link to how others treat you based on your attitude that defines you. Are other people tolerant of you, or do they view you as intolerant largely because of your attitude toward life, situations, and other people?

Many believe that in the business world, after nonperformance,

a poor attitude is the next leading reason why many individuals are fired. A converse belief states that for qualified individuals, a positive can-do attitude may be the predominate reason why individuals gain and maintain roles and jobs. Your attitude has the power to allow others to tolerate you or view you as intolerable.

The effect of being tolerable extends beyond the business world. Some individuals have begun and experienced excellent careers and relationships with others based on possessing an outstanding attitude. Caution: do not be fooled into thinking that your bosses or circle of personal friends will not "fire" you once they perceive you as intolerable. Some may give you a verbal warning and others may place you on probation in their mind. Some may immediately have you looking for another circle to join if you do not have a great deal of goodwill tolerance accumulated. Use your attitude to create great amounts of tolerance. You do not want to find yourself on the outside of your chosen circle.

I.

The "I" in A.T.T.I.T.U.D.E. refers to *inspiration* and the power to inspire others. Inspiration can operate in your favor for you internally and externally. A positive attitude inspires you to believe in who you are, what you can positively affect right now, and what you can do in the future. How many talented, bright, dynamic, yet uninspired individuals do you see underachieve in what they are capable of because of a lack of inspiration? I believe that inspiration and motivation differ. At the same time, they are related. While many factors may serve as motivation for us, we must be inspired to act on a motivating factor.

A properly positioned attitude enables each of us to look at people and situations in a manner that uplifts and propels us forward. As previously stated, this is not an attempt to get you to buy into *feel-good* rhetoric and believe that every situation is full of positive information. Life does not happen that way. On the contrary, it is my desire that you understand that your ability to move forward will often be predicated on your ability to find some level of inspiration in

whatever you encounter, based on your attitude.

We know that people and our experiences shape our attitude. Are you in healthy situations that inspire you toward developing and maintaining a positive attitude regarding your present situation and your future? As far as you can control it, do you seek to surround yourself with people who inspire you toward your destiny? With your attitude as your filter, are you getting closer to walking in the purpose for your life? These are important questions that you are best suited to answer. If we take the concept of inspiration beyond ourselves, each of us should look to inspire other people. How inspiring are you, and can others look to you as a source of positive inspiration? If the answer is a resounding "no," could it be that your attitude is preventing it from happening? I encourage you to be an inspiration to someone, even as you seek inspiration from others and situations.

T.

For the third time, we will deal with the letter T. This time around; T represents *tenacity,* as it relates to attitude. A positive, can-do attitude should produce a level of tenacity within you that enables you to exemplify resilience toward your goals when challenges are close and the finish line appears far away. The power of a can-do attitude will help you maintain focus and stay steadfast in your resolve when the going gets rough.

There is an often-told story of a man who became separated from his hiking party in the woods on a winter evening. After a few hours passed, the temperature dropped slightly, and fatigue began to descend on him. His outlook regarding his situation began to sink, and he eventually accepted the fact that he would not survive the night. After walking for miles, the man decided that he would not walk any farther and abandoned the prospect of finding his party. He gave up on the possibility that anyone would find him in time to rescue him. He did not have enough tenacity for his survival. The next morning, a farmer found the man just over a small ridge only one hundred yards away from the farmhouse. The lost hiker was unconscious and

extremely frostbitten after a night on the cold ground. In addition to the weather being a danger, a bear or wolf could have discovered him during the night. Although he survived and eventually recovered, his lack of tenacity to survive kept him separated from the nearby warm farmhouse. It was the hiker's attitude that caused him to give up when met with the challenge of getting to safety.

Most of us, fortunately, will not have to endure a situation this extreme. Closer to home, how many times have we given up on an important task at hand or strayed from our designated path because our attitude did not support the level of tenacity we needed to endure? In many instances, success and positive outcomes are just ahead or over the next hill. We are often closer than we think, and if we only kept going, we would find our brand of safety and success. Does your attitude provide you with resilience to endure challenging people so that you are not knocked off your desired trajectory through life? Even if someone does not knock you off of your path, do you have time for someone to delay you from your purpose? Your key to moving forward may lie in your attitude and how you leverage your positive attitude to remain tenacious through the negative.

U.

The U in our acronym represents *understanding*. Much has been written around the ancient discussion to seek the meaning of life. You will likely receive a unique response from each person you choose to question regarding his or her perspective of the meaning of life. Some may adamantly profess to have the answer to this deep question. Let me make this declaration: you will not find the answer to that question within this book. The reason I bring up this question is that it is one that seeks an ultimate understanding of all that transpires around us. Your attitude should position you to develop an understanding of what is going on around you and how to emerge from situations and interactions with others. A positive attitude should prompt each of us to seek to understand why we are here and what we can achieve on our journey through life. In seeking our individual understanding, it

is necessary to ask critical questions along the way.

Does your attitude prompt you to ask the right questions? Are you the one who always seeks to understand why bad breaks and adverse situations always seem to happen to you, or are you the one who seeks to understand the lessons that can be learned from situations? The longer I live, the more I understand the value and benefit of listening to gain essential understanding from other people. The degree to which I can listen and learn is greatly affected by my attitude toward the individual or the situation. You may not be much different from me in this respect. I am willing to bet that your perspective is greatly affected by your attitude toward the people and situations you encounter.

This writing is not all about how to overcome the negative. A positive attitude can help you maintain the right perspective and help you move forward with greater impact. There is a great deal to learn when situations and interactions with others go well. Be just as critical in seeking to understand what went well when you enjoy a positive outcome. How will you comprehend how to replicate favorable outcomes without an understanding of what enabled your success? A positive attitude should spark a level of intellectual curiosity that leads you to greater understanding through the good and the bad. View your ability to understand your attitude as your internal GPS to keep you on track and on pace to arrive at your destination.

D.

The letter D represents the concept of *determination*. Previously I wrote about the importance of resiliency. Determination is a similar thought and essential to leveraging a positive attitude. Your level of determination in simple language is your demonstrated effort toward accomplishing what you have declared as important and worthwhile achieving. I will intentionally stress the importance of indicating that there is great value in recognizing that your self-declaration is essential with this point. Other people and the gravity of certain situations may establish high priorities for us throughout our journey through

life. It may be easy to say that we have a sense of determination. Saying it is important, for there is amazing power in what we speak. We know that words alone do not accomplish the task at hand and we must take concerted action. Often when we begin to take action, challenges arise, frustration becomes a factor, and we may even lose our direction.

Although we may temporarily lose our way, determination fueled by a positive attitude is what will keep us focused and moving forward. It is not a matter of whether challenges and setbacks come. In most instances, the real question is when opposition shows up, how will we react, and how will we address it? In the field of behavioral psychiatry, fight or flight mechanism describes the stress response that our bodies exhibit when faced with threatening situations. While in survival mode, we either confront our threats or run away from threats. What is your response when challenges and setbacks threaten your desired levels of success? Are you one who fights and confronts your challenges, or does the notion of delay and opposition send you running for cover? A positive attitude can arm you with the determination needed to press beyond challenges and opposition.

A direct effect of moving forward in a determined manner is an increase in your confidence level. When you employ a no-quit perspective to overcome challenges, it is hard not to realize a surge in self-confidence. Real determination has demonstrated proof points. Your proof points become evidence that you have not chosen to flee. **You are in the fight to learn the lesson and to move forward in a positive manner.** Determination may be described as "grit" or, simply stated, a level of resolve whereby nothing thing of this earth can turn you away. Typically, one only demonstrates this level of determination when one's attitude is aligned with one's goals and efforts required to achieve success.

E.

The final letter in our A.T.T.I.T.U.D.E. acronym is E, which represents *empowered*. A positive attitude can serve as a tool to propel

you to successful relationships with other people and toward successful outcomes in situations you encounter. Up to this point, I have discussed many virtues and benefits of possessing a positive attitude. I have not taken time to capture all this information for you to learn and not do anything with it. A strong sense of empowerment will help you move forward with what you are reading. If you are already doing much of what I have captured, congratulations! You may be well on your way. Regardless of whether this is your first effort to understand and leverage a positive attitude or if you have been at this task for some time, most of us have an opportunity to improve. Feeling empowered to make a difference will serve you well in doing so.

Life has a way of wearing each of us down, and I am not exempt from this happening. If we are not careful, we welcome people into our lives who wear us down and take away our momentum unnecessarily. Our experiences and interactions with others often create memories within us that cause us to act and react to situations in ways that are not supportive of a positive attitude.

I am reminded of a story I learned of about an individual who observed trained elephants walking in line with each animal held only by a simple rope tied to its ankle. Elephants are intelligent animals with a highly defined social order. They are known for having a great memory. What intrigued the observer was the fact that there were no heavy ropes or chains required to restrain the powerful beasts. The trainer explained that from the time the elephants are very young and begin training, they are forcibly tied down by connecting a rope to their ankle, and they are not able to move or pull away. This experience is very traumatic; it changes the juvenile elephant's view of freedom to the point that it no longer feels empowered to roam. The young elephants grew up with their sense of empowerment forever stripped from them. Mature elephants trained in this manner are no longer a threat to overpower handlers or roam independently as long as the rope remained tied to the elephant's ankle.

Now, you may ask what does this story have to do with my attitude? I am happy that you asked me this question! Just as young

elephants endure traumatic training and conditioning, your life experiences and adverse interactions with people can have the same effect on you. Without realizing it, you can become stripped of your sense of empowerment and power to move forward in the direction you desire. Later, even when negative influences are absent, you may behave as the trained elephants behaved and remain constrained by a proverbial rope, which truthfully has no power to constrain you from success. What situations and interactions are you allowing to make a negative imprint on your attitude? Do you feel that you have the ability to recognize when these negative experiences begin to feed your mind and memory with information you would rather not focus on? Once those undesirable experiences permeate your mental lines of defense, you may find yourself tied to the negative, which prevents you from focusing on what is important to move forward in a positive manner. What is holding you down, and what is attempting to rob you of your ability to move freely? If you had to make a list, what serves as the "rope" tied to your ankle in your life?

I encourage you to use a positive attitude to sever whatever rope may exist or use it to prevent the adverse and metaphorical rope from being attached to you. Use a positive attitude to remain empowered to build high-quality relationships and affect situations in a positive way. Do all you can to prevent others from looking at you and saying, "It is hard to believe that she is not more successful in achieving the purpose and dreams she often discusses." Ensure that observations of you do not include the fact that though you possess great power, potential, and ability, you consistently miss the mark. Make sure your storyline includes all of the details of how you used your positive attitude to remain empowered to take action. Do not aimlessly follow the crowd bound by ropes of negativity.

Develop and nurture your sense of empowerment and maintain a positive attitude. Use a positive attitude as your personal launching pad to propel you into the stratosphere for success as you define it. Why aim for the clouds when you've prepared for interplanetary travel? Unleash your power and soar. **You must believe that you are**

empowered and then act with empowered purpose. Your attitude is essential when taking this approach. Unleash your power and soar.

Attitude is a more than just a word. Maximize your use of all that accompanies your attitude. Each word represented by the A.T.T.I.T.U.D.E. acronym represents your personal recipe for success. Whether you consider trust, inspiration, empowerment, or any of the concepts discussed, it is up to you to determine how to incorporate each element into your DNA. When you apply each concept in harmony with one another, you will be on your way to living a life defined by a positive attitude.

Affirmation #8

I affirm that I will empower A.T.T.I.T.U.D.E. in all that I do.

CHAPTER 9

Leveraging Success and Building a Positive Track Record

"Whether you think you can or think you can't, you're right."
—Henry Ford

If you were to speak with individuals who have achieved a demonstrated level of consistent success in life, they would likely state that the ability to understand what it took to become successful was paramount. There are countless stories of so-called "instant champions" or individuals and organizations that stumbled into success. There are many examples of "one-hit wonders" who achieved a moment of success. However, they were not able to demonstrate the ability to maintain being on top of the world. Most of the time, success and positive outcomes are the results of consistently doing what is necessary to create success.

Understanding and leveraging your attitude to create successful outcomes in your life follows the same path. Each of us must first understand the circumstances and conditions whereby our attitude is at its very best. We must understand what makes us a winner and what creates positive attitudinal outcomes to replicate the same level of success in future interactions. We see this play out in many situations daily. If you are a golf fan, watch your favorite player, and you will see a consistent routine each time that the player approaches the tee

or when the player attempts a relatively easy twelve-foot putt. Some business leaders engage in the same routine each morning when they have to deliver an important presentation to senior executives or the board of directors. Parents often employ a consistent routine when running the gauntlet to make it out of the house in the morning to make it to school on time.

The point that I am making is that once you understand what it takes to create a positive outcome, you are in a much better position to be able to replicate those same conditions for another win. Do conditions change? They do, and as we already know by now, many things are outside of our control. This will always be the case. I am writing of the conditions and scenarios you can control that will affect your outcome. This chapter is written to help you understand the best ways to leverage the wins involved with who you are based on your attitude. Once you master this principle, your attitudinal wins become your résumé of past success and your playbook for interactions in the future. Let us begin!

I want you to think about a time when something happened to you that was truly unpleasant. Perhaps it was an interaction with an individual or something that took place at school or on the job. Do not just select any unpleasant situation, concentrate on one when the way that you handled the situation made all the difference in the world. I knew it would not take you too long to come up with an example. Although faced with a scenario you either did not like or did not enjoy, you persevered and came through it with positivity intact. How did you make it through, and what past experiences did you extract that helped you achieve a positive outcome? Perhaps you were not thinking about it in the specific terms that I am using now. Very likely you were doing your best just to make it through your challenge and did not think about how your experience was preparing you for the future. If my assumption is correct, that is fine and is not intended to sound judgmental at all. I want to help you develop a pattern of reflecting on scenarios that went well for you. Yes, there are lessons that each of us should learn when we do not win or when outcomes

are not favorable for us. Since our goal is a positive attitude, I want to focus on harnessing power identified when your positive attitude made a difference. Let us examine history through a simple exercise to capture a collection of positive outcomes. If you guessed another checkup is on the way, you are correct.

Attitudinal Checkup VIII: Your Positive History

- ❖ List three to five scenarios or events that provided major lessons learned regarding how to navigate less-than-positive situations.
- ❖ In those situations, or when you encountered a challenging person, were there any common positive thoughts that enabled you to overcome the situation?
- ❖ In your reflection, identify and describe times when you chose not to engage in a negative manner that made a difference when you had positive outcomes.
- ❖ Were there any techniques that you remember that you can call on in the future when you face difficult people or that you may use in challenging situations?
- ❖ Identify and describe common strengths used that empowered you to move from a positive attitude to positive consequences.

Document your findings; oftentimes a visible reminder is great mental training and visual conditioning that creates routines that help us. This simple exercise is one you can use periodically to accelerate your learning curve through life's challenges.

I intentionally asked you to consider scenarios from your past to make my concepts real and relevant to your life story. None of my writing will resonate with you until you can personalize the message. None of my words are believable or of value if you are not able to make a connection to your experiences. It is imperative for you to have a tool or system to identify successes to remember them and call on them when needed. In a previous chapter, I used an example

of how a golfer steps up to the tee with confidence, looks downrange toward the hole, then swings with the best stroke possible. Much of what you see take place are habits and routines born out of understanding what it takes to hit the ball from the tee successfully. **Remember this: Mistakes and successes yield teachable moments!** This concept extends far beyond the golf course. Just as the golfer learned, there are myriad situations when we can demonstrate how understanding lessons learned enabled us to improve performance. A great question to ask yourself always is this: What am I learning from this teachable moment?

Understanding and building a positive track record is the paramount foundation to generating positive attitudinal outcomes and positive consequences. I suggest that you do not underestimate the value of understanding the dynamics of situations and people, which is the beginning of understanding how you present yourself in those situations and to others. Will you always understand everything? Of course not; however, the more you engage in thoughtful reflection, the more you increase your chances to understand the process of consistently engaging with a positive attitude. This sort of thoughtful reflection becomes important when establishing your positive track record. When you engage in thoughtful reflection, you can tap into positive proof points from the core of who you are.

Once we take the time to understand the factors that enable our successes, we can recall what we did and apply those same practices in future scenarios. Accumulating your personalized storehouse of success strategies birthed from thoughtful analysis of how you positively navigated through challenging situations places you on a path for future successes. Volumes of literature written by scholars and scientists argue that success breeds success. Others argue that success is the result of hard work and making excellent decisions. I will not make the choice of solely aligning my thoughts and opinions exclusively with either position. I do believe that regardless of how one defines a successful outcome in a given situation, reaching that point requires a mix of several factors, including excellent decision making,

employing resilience, and beginning a pattern of early successes. The same approach works with your attitude. How you approach situations and people has an effect on your attitude. The choices you make and the data points you choose to remember affects your attitude. Lastly, previous successes that you can recall at a later time may indeed affect your attitude. Do not become distracted by my use of the word *early* when describing success. Some of us have been at this wonderful blessing called life for longer than others. Just as we can teach an old(er) dog new tricks, we can benefit from learning some of life's lessons later in our journey.

The ability to recall useful information has great value in most areas of life. The ability to recall previous attitudinal success may prove to be a game-changer within your life. Consider how much power and capacity for success you maintain when you have a reliable system that quickly recalls what is most useful to help you approach situations with a positive attitude. Why give all your power and ability away by approaching scenarios and people with the wrong attitude? The system you take the time to develop can become your means of recalling previous successes and using that same knowledge to go forward.

Previously I asked you to document factors and situations when you approached challenging situations and your attitude made a difference. Lessons learned from that exercise are now a part of your system. Take the time to seek feedback from others regarding how you handled specific situations. Feedback provided may become a part of the data in your system. I encourage you to leverage technology. If listening to positive messaging and motivational information by podcast or streaming on your smart device is useful, then utilize your technology as a part of your system. Scholars have studied and written vast amounts of facts and opinions about the impact repetition has on learning. You may not believe that practice makes perfect, but our goal is a path of continual improvement, as opposed to perfection. Besides, who on this earth has a perfect attitude? Very likely no one at all. There are those, however, who have conditioned their

minds to approach just about every situation or person in a positive manner that is empowering.

As you progress through this book, you may not currently have a reliable system or a means to recall your successes. A reliable system or means to recall successes adds value when developing your positive track record. Ideally you will emerge from this chapter realizing the value of creating your system with a sense of urgency to apply it. You have the capacity to do so. I will step back and use the imagery of a bodybuilder to make my point. Individuals more mature in this process may look like attitudinal bodybuilders with developed routines, practices, and consistent methods to deal with all that life throws in their direction. You too have the capacity to learn and leverage the same level of discipline. The fact that you feel you are a lightweight now is no reason to delay building those muscles for growth and greater stability. Your muscle system is essentially important to your body's health and wellbeing. The same holds true for your positive attitude and the system in place to maintain a positive perspective and approach to life. Flex those muscles, challenge yourself, get plenty of rest, and consistently move towards improvement. I encourage you to tap into your positive track record and leverage it in future situations. Create the level of success with your attitude that you wish to replicate. Remember, this technique aligns with the process of leveraging your personal successes to develop your positive track record. In the next chapter, I will go further and discuss putting the pieces together for your benefit.

Affirmation #9

I affirm that each day I will continuously build on my track record of positive attitudinal successes.

CHAPTER 10

How Will You Be Defined?

Your positive attitude will prevent negative people and adverse events from getting the best of you.

At this point in our journey, my hope is that you now have a greater understanding of your attitude and how important it is for each of us to command a positive attitude when facing all that life and people throw our way. A major motivation for my writing and sharing my thoughts was to create meaningful dialogue with you regarding this important topic. Attitude affects everyone, and everyone possesses an attitude. No one is exempt. On the surface, that idea may not sound like a positive notion. How often do you hear someone say, "You have an attitude"? When you hear that declaration about you, how do you react? Did the sound of that statement make you defensive? Were you on edge and ready to pounce? I am willing to suggest that when you heard it, you could tell by the tone of the person speaking whether your attitude was viewed as positive or negative. Did you become defensive? Did you fire back, "No, I'm not the one with an attitude problem."? Did you immediately turn the table to express to the other person how much you thought that *he* or *she* had an attitude? The reality is that we all have attitudes. Every one of us has an attitude in any given moment and at every waking moment of the day.

Pay close attention to my next few words. This may come as a

shock to you: ***the attitude you possess at any given moment is the attitude you selected.*** You own your attitude, and taking it was your choice. No one forced you to select it. Situations and circumstances may influence how you view particular events and occurrences. Your history with an individual may affect future interactions with the same individual or with others. This is not rocket science; you chose your attitude, and you hold the deed of ownership. When your attitude is positive and you bring value to those around you, your disposition enables you to enjoy all the positive benefits that come along with owning such a valuable asset. Conversely, when you possess a negative, counterproductive or destructive attitude, you own all the negative consequences that come along with that deed of ownership.

The important choices we make when we decide what informs our attitude becomes the foundation for how we define ourselves. In many instances, other people use that same information, as it manifests in our attitude, to define how they view us and how they relate to us.

Based on your attitude, how will you define yourself? What type of experiences do you convey when others interact with you that enables them to define you? I will cover this subject from two separate angles. First, I will spend time considering how you choose to define yourself, and then we will examine how others may define us based on our attitude.

To understand who we are and what shapes how we define ourselves, we must begin at the core of who we are. Whether we consciously think about it or not, each of us has a certain worldview. People's worldviews are an extremely complex combination of factors and the culmination of the effects of events they have experienced. These factors and events shape individuals' perspective of their existence and how they interpret all that occurs around them. In simplistic terms, individuals' worldviews become a portal of how they see the world and the events and interactions they are a part of. The manner in which individuals experience life events and situations affects their worldview. An individuals' worldview comes about as a result of synthesis that takes place in their mind and how they

feel about the events and people they encounter either directly or indirectly. The opinions and perspectives that each of us possesses influence and affect how we observe the universe around us and how we define ourselves.

I will return to our progressive model to support my point regarding one's worldview and the link to how we define ourselves.

The Infinity Attitude Cycle

An individual's worldview is a major contributor to that individual's attitude. For example, how people feel about their physical environment may affect their worldview. The way people feel about the treatment of certain groups of people affects their worldview. Individuals' experience of interacting with other people affects their worldview, especially if they believe that many other similar people act or behave in the same manner. The perception that people emerge with as a result of their life experiences becomes a reality to them, whether the perception is accurate or not. In following the path of the model, the resulting attitude that is formed in part by one's worldview drives that person's thoughts, actions, and outcomes and ultimately creates the set of consequences that the person must deal with.

The manner in which we choose to react and become influenced by all that we encounter can shape and form the definition that we place on ourselves and the way we see ourselves in this world. True to our prevailing theme of defining ourselves by attitude, each of us must serve as a gatekeeper and manage how our worldview influences our attitude and what type of person we choose to be, based on the manner in which we act and think borne out of our worldview. A positive attitude toward life, derived from our worldview, typically leads to positive thinking, positive actions, positive outcomes, and beneficial (positive) outcomes. The same path and progression takes

place with negative inputs and has the real potential to lead to adverse consequences.

We experience cycles of life in myriad ways, and sometimes we react differently to the same types of events and occurrences based on when we encounter them. Timing becomes crucial. How we feel at any given moment influences how we choose to internalize our experiences. As a reminder, life is not always pleasant, and important events do not always occur sequentially in an ideal manner. However events play out in your life, you must choose how you react and how those inputs inform your attitude. This behavior becomes an essential part of the way you choose to define who you are.

As I move on to my second angle to deal with this topic, our model does not change drastically. Our worldview continues to serve as a major contributor to our attitude, thoughts, actions, outcomes, and consequences. The difference in our discussion now shifts away from the manner that we choose to define ourselves and shifts toward how others may choose to define us. At this point, I hope that the progression of the model is thoroughly understood, and I will not lay out an extended example to restate the premise of the model. The major difference is that other people have the ability to render judgment on each of us based on the attitude we choose. Others observe our actions we display as a result of our thoughts. You already know where I am going; these actions produce outcomes and resulting consequences. Take a moment and step back to consider all the data points that each of us provides others that they may use to analyze how they choose to define us. Several relevant questions emerge for each of us to consider as we contemplate how other people choose to define us.

- ❖ What is my worldview, and how do I allow what is going on around me to influence my attitude?
- ❖ Do I typically internalize negative or positive aspects of my life experiences?
- ❖ Do I pursue a positive or negative attitude to guide my thinking and the origin of my actions?

- ❖ Am I typically satisfied with the outcomes of my actions?
- ❖ Do I see an opportunity to create improved outcomes by choosing to begin my cycle with a positive attitude?

I did not establish those questions as an Attitudinal Checkup; however, I did want to pause for you to think about a few important concepts. No need to worry; there will be additional Checkups in our journey ahead.

Here is a timely caveat relevant to our discussion, and it serves as a partial review of chapter four. In case you forgot or do not wish to flip back, in chapter four I focused on the question of "What can I control?" We are assured by now that we cannot control other individuals. Just as we make conscious decisions regarding how we feel about all that takes place around us, others do the same. Other people come to conclusions based on their life experiences, which includes their interactions and engagements with us. **How someone else chooses to feel about you is out of your control.** Make sure you take special note of what ideally is an obvious thought by now. Regardless of how much you may wish to change this fact, you cannot. What you can control is how you choose to inform your attitude, which leads to outcomes. Based on how you progress through your personal model, beginning with your attitude, provides you with an incredible opportunity to influence how other people choose to define you.

In the physical world, many individuals believe in the laws of attraction. Simply stated, some believe that positivity attracts positivity and that negativity attracts negativity. The same analogy ties into the importance of defining ourselves with a positive attitude and influencing others to do the same. Countless times we observe how some people let an adverse event or interaction provide adverse information that informs their attitude. Before long, here comes the negative thoughts, and before they people realize it, they are dealing with adverse outcomes on the back end. To top matters off, in many instances the initial event or engagement that the individuals viewed as problematic and

adopted was not even a challenge or issue for them to deal with. Be sure to understand the following point: **As gatekeeper, always be aware not to take on problems and challenges that are not yours but that have the ability to taint your attitude.** *Pick and choose wisely before taking on battles that do not belong to you.* How will you recognize that selecting an inappropriate battle and adopting it as your own is the very distraction that could permanently take you from the path to achieving your true purpose in life? Do you want to take the risk?

According to the laws of attraction, all of the negativity that you choose to associate yourself with will attract only greater amounts of negativity; hence the cliché "Misery loves company." Conversely, when individuals make intentional choices to associate with positive perspectives and allows those positive perspectives to become absorbed into the core of who they are as a person, they are more likely to attract positive experiences and enjoy a greater number of positive engagements. Make wise decisions regarding which battles you choose to adopt as your own. In some scenarios, it may be wise to avoid unnecessary battles altogether if you have that option.

I will now introduce you to Martina as an example of how the laws of attraction may work against you. Martina worked for a large organization and was pleasant and outgoing. She had a great personality, delivered results at a high level, and was well-liked by many individuals in the organization. One Monday morning Martina overheard a few fellow employees expressing displeasure over an event that took place over the weekend. Martina watched the news the night before and was aware of the controversial issue and had an opinion regarding the event. Deep down inside, Martina sympathized with those adversely affected by what took place; however, she decided to remain silent whenever anyone nearby brought up the event as a discussion topic. She was concerned that she might say the wrong words or that her opinion would not be accepted by those with whom she enjoyed great professional relationships. What Martina did in response to the event created a longer-lasting, adverse reaction among those from whom she desired to hide her words and thoughts.

Martina's worldview and personal relationships with several coworkers informed her attitude regarding what took place and the public opinion surrounding the event. Because of her change in attitude, Martina's thoughts shifted, and she began to think differently about those who were victimized during the weekend's activities. She not only began to think differently, Martina also began to treat a few individuals differently because of her change in attitude regarding the alleged perpetrators and victims involved in the incident. You may have some thoughts of how this turn of events changed several relationships in Martina's life. The actions that she began taking represented a departure from the type of person that she had always represented herself to be. This behavior created dramatically different outcomes for Martina, and she was not welcomed among some of her longtime friends. In the minds of some, Martina did not suddenly become some horrible beast to avoid at all cost. When they became aware of her new attitude, thoughts, and actions, they began to engage in conversations differently with Martina and kept certain communications away from her, which would have never happened in the past. To complete walking through our model, Martina suffered not knowing about several important events and activities on the horizon that she normally would have known about. Additionally, word began to spread around the office, and whenever the topic surfaced, many individuals quickly associated Martina with one of the sides represented in the conflict.

Let's take a minute to understand what took place. The incident neither was of great importance to Martina nor did it directly affect her in any manner. Martina was entitled to develop an opinion of what happened. It was the results of what became her actions that positioned Martina in an undesirable place among her coworkers. It was perceived that Martina aligned with what many viewed as the negative side of the situation. As time passed, other individuals began to associate her with adverse elements associated with the event. In this scenario, it appears as though the laws of attraction worked against Martina. She was not a negative person; however, one could

reason that she aligned herself with a less than positive event which affected her actions. This is an example of what may happen when we adopt battles that we never intended to fight or when we associate ourselves unnecessarily with negativity. I am not advocating that we should move through life as emotionless beings without compassion for others. I am also not suggesting that you become someone you are not or fail to address conflict when necessary. Be your authentic self and stand up for your values and opinions whereas they represent who you are as a person. I am suggesting that we should judiciously determine how, where and when we engage, if we are given a choice.

It is critically important that we make wise decisions regarding how all that takes place around us affects our attitude. How will we choose to define ourselves? What will we place into the atmosphere around us that will influence how other individuals define us? Remember from previous discussions that we own our attitude **100%** and all that comes along with it. Martina could not control how others perceived her actions. She could control only her reaction to the activities that played out over the weekend. Looking at her situation from an ownership perspective, Martina had a significant influence on how her coworkers began to define her existence.

Martina represents a single individual within a specific scenario. How many times have you seen others fall into the same pattern and follow a similar course of action? How many of us have done something similar? This setup is not as far-fetched as it may sound. My desire is to bring it to your awareness to keep you from falling into the same potentially adverse patterns. If scenarios like this have happened to you more often than you care to remember, make this your day to begin to inspect how you typically handle situations and reevaluate your path. It is hard work and requires intentional effort. In being 100% transparent, I am not just writing about this subject to fill the pages. I too must employ an intentional effort to avoid battles I was not intended to fight, and I must consider the implication of permitting adverse events from informing my attitude in a manner that is unhealthy for me.

You may want to reread this chapter at some point in your future. These thoughts are at the core of our attitude discussion for what I hope are obvious reasons. Choose wisely and do your best to influence the definition of who you are in a positive manner. Do you define yourself as one who attracts the negatives from life in the same way that a strong magnet pulls nails from a box? Conversely, do you define yourself as an individual who brings positivity and a *can-do* attitude to all you are engaged in? Is your very presence best described as a repugnant odor or a breath of fresh air? Will the manner in which you define yourself cause others to refer to you as one who sees possibilities, or are you "the dream killer?" You can make positives happen in a big way. You may need some practice, which becomes your path to improvement. In our next chapter, I will spend some time discussing what to do with the definition of who you are that you are working hard construct. Take a moment or two and digest this chapter (do not take too long) and get ready to forge ahead.

Affirmation #10

I affirm that I will define myself and do my very best to influence how others define me through the attitude I possess and showcase to the world.

CHAPTER **11**

Applying Your Definition through Your Touch Points

Moving through life without leveraging positivity as a tool is much like driving into the forest to cut down a tree while leaving your axe and chainsaw at home in your garage.

Welcome back, and I trust that your time away was not too long. Take a moment and once again congratulate yourself for continuing your journey through my writing. I applaud your commitment toward mastering your attitude, which can change who you are and change your life. Additionally, I trust that you are now in a better position to recognize attitudinal patterns that come to life in your interactions with others. This knowledge can enhance the way you engage with other people. Remember, you cannot control others, and they cannot control you. Knowledge of how this dynamic plays out should serve as a powerful asset for your use.

Know that defining yourself by your attitude and committing to improve is an ongoing effort. There are no days off, and endless are the opportunities for you to present either a positive or negative attitude to the world. This thought is not intended to be depressing. The great news is that if you are consciously working through how and when you deal with your engagements, you are already blessed and

alive with the opportunity to make a positive difference. Applying all you are learning is valuable to you. I am confident you value working hard to understand who you are and how you may positively affect others through your attitude. I am confident by now that when someone approaches you with the comment "You have an attitude," you are now more than ready to positively respond and walk them through our model, fully explaining how your positive attitude affects your thoughts, actions, outcomes, and consequences in a positive way. OK, you may not have *that* much time available. If you do, you are now armed to begin that conversation.

In a previous chapter, I spent some time navigating through examples of how a negative attitude can "sink" how we choose to define ourselves and adversely affect our ability to influence how others define us. Our goal is to create positive attitudinal currency that gives each of us heightened spending ability on our journey through life. All the time devoted toward understanding and defining who you are through your attitude was not meant to create a tool to place on the shelf or use on a limited basis. We must be able to apply our definition to our lives, for this positive concept to be successful.

Merely believing that you have a positive attitude or working hard to develop a positive attitude is not enough. For maximum life benefit, it is now time to move our discussion into the phase to cover what constitutes useful application. Think of your attitude as a tool or a guide that has amazing power and influence on your life. I will tell a brief story to illustrate the impact of what can happen when we fail to use valuable tools available to us.

Paul was an accomplished contractor and labored many years perfecting his craft as a home designer and homebuilder. His talents were amazing, and customers were always extremely satisfied with his exquisite houses and finely crafted works. While building these fantastic homes, Paul was a stickler for using all the proper tools at his disposal. In fact, he once stated that without his tools there was no way he could have made much progress and certainly could not have completed a house that could stand up to his high-quality standards.

Additionally, without his valuable tools, such a dwelling would not have met his client's expectations. Paul spent many years enjoying the benefits of what could be accomplished when he properly used his tools. Somewhere along the way, Paul's confidence got the best of him, and he changed a few of his homebuilding routines. There were instances when he relied on an "eye-test" to determine length, as opposed to using a tape measure, prior to cutting materials. On occasion Paul estimated how much water to add to certain ingredients that required mixing, instead of measuring specific amounts. More than once, he experienced inconsistencies when completing tasks by hand while he ignored opportunities to use power tools to complete the homes he built.

I hope you are able to see where I am going. Paul, though extremely accomplished, failed to maintain the routine of using his valuable tools. His successes and accomplishments were well documented and substantial, yet he did not maintain an established discipline to his craft. Over time, his reputation as a high-quality homebuilder suffered and he was faced with deciding whether he had what it took to continue building homes. All of the time and efforts that Paul invested into creating a reputation as an extraordinary builder was lost in his decisions not to use the tools at his disposal. Potential buyers lost faith and confidence in his abilities. Eventually Paul was forced to walk away from his craft. This example may seem an extreme one to show what can happen when tools are abandoned or when one chooses to "wing it" and make important decisions in the absence of the very items that contributed to success in a major way. After all, Paul's *capacity* to deliver fine quality homes did not change, but his *ability* to deliver fine quality homes diminished through conscious decisions to forgo using the right tools.

Let's return to our discussion of a positive attitude and revive the notion of how choosing positivity is an extremely valuable tool in our lives. Up to this point I have focused on understanding the impact, consequences, and benefits of what possessing a positive attitude can mean to each of us. Ideally, you are now convinced how you wish to

define yourself and how you wish for others to define you through the attitude you choose. Your attitude is a priceless tool at your disposal, and as Paul did, you have the ability to create amazing outcomes through the use of your tool. With this asset in your toolbox, why would one choose to "wing it," when it comes to approaching situations and people while ignoring the value of a positive attitude? It may be easy to observe and critique Paul for making decisions to ignore using the proper tools. He was an accomplished homebuilder, a professional. How many times have we intentionally or unintentionally made decisions in the absence of a positive attitude as our tool?

How we choose to define ourselves through our attitude is a very personal choice. I am thinking that if you are still reading, your desire is to define yourself with a positive attitude or at the least understand the value of a positive disposition. After developing your tool, you must use it. I exercise caution and try to neither oversimplify topics nor make overly complex statements. In this instance, realizing the positive power of your attitude as your tool is as close as applying your chosen definition of a positive attitude.

Imagine yourself as the latest and greatest superhero on the market! You may not have the ability to fly, you may not bend steel with your bare hands or burn a hole through solid lead with your heat vision. I doubt you are able to become invisible or outrun a speeding bullet. The superpower and heightened ability you now possess is your positive attitude. After all of your introspective thinking, you are now ready to take on the world. You have invested valuable effort into understanding the benefits and detriments that await you based on how you define yourself through your attitude.

In our daily walk, we have the ability to make a difference through our engagements and touchpoints with others. Countless situations and events provide us with the opportunity to make a positive difference. Now is a great time to briefly review our model.

The Infinity Attitude Cycle

The path to success remains consistent. By beginning with a positive attitude and progressing to positive consequences using your super power, you can make a difference. When you make the choice to select a positive approach to life, you position yourself to move down the path of positive thoughts and actions. Ideally when we make this choice we are in a much better place to create positive outcomes and enjoy the corresponding consequences and benefits. You are now armed with information that will help you recognize this pattern as one you wish to repeat in order to take advantage of positive life momentum as a result of your attitude. As the saying goes, success breeds success.

Consider the interactions you have with those closest to you or those you spend the greatest amount of time interacting with on a regular basis. Whether interaction occurs primarily with family members or with your team in business situations, your attitude is critical, and you can make a positive impact. Using your attitude as your valuable tool, consider how future interactions will be different based on applying a positive point of view and a can-do perspective. Your lens of life absolutely has the ability to add incremental value to those closest to you through the positive interactions you have with them. Do not underestimate the power you now possess. Remember, I already bestowed super-hero status on you a few paragraphs ago.

Consider your new world where you enjoy many more positive outcomes and benefits of interactions with those you spend great amounts of time with, because you made the decision to approach life with greater positivity, armed with an uplifting attitude. You cannot control others; however, you may exercise greater positive influence on how they perceive and define you through your attitude. At this point, take a moment to think about a conversation or interaction

with someone close that had a less than desirable outcome. While we know we cannot control others, how might that same interaction have turned out differently based on changing only a single factor in the equation—**YOU**? How could a different attitude have caused different thoughts about that person? Based on different thoughts, are you able to determine that you may have chosen a different course of actions with different outcomes? The prize at the end of the cycle might have been valuable benefits and consequences that all began with a change in your attitude.

The same positive pattern can play out in other areas of your life. What projects or initiatives do you touch in your career wherein your attitude alone can make a great difference? What routine tasks do you complete that would not seem nearly as onerous if you were simply to improve your attitude and change your approach to making progress toward completion? Where do you volunteer your time in an effort to serve others? Although your engagement is likely a worthwhile activity and others probably benefit greatly from your involvement, how could you improve the experience by taking a more positive attitude? Think about one of your trademark comments or remarks that somehow "slipped" out of your mouth that should never have entered your mind. How might a change in attitude serve as an effective gatekeeper to prevent you from taking conversations to a place where they should not go? I want to be sure you fully understand why leading with a positive attitude is necessary for you and how others perceive you. Managing your persona through your attitude is a matter of personal brand management. You are the owner of your brand, and it all begins with the attitude you possess. I am the owner of my brand and thus I am not exempt from this concept. In personalizing this message, I am bound to the same concepts that I am writing about, and I understand the super power I possess through my attitude.

I will now ask you to internalize these concepts through the following checkup. It has been a while since the previous checkup, and I want to be sure to maintain your attention.

Attitudinal Checkup IX: Inspecting Your Touch Points

- ❖ How do you feel about looking at your critical touch points with others, and what are a few of the attitudinal shifts you are willing to make to improve how future interactions with these individuals may occur?
- ❖ What are some of the ways you are now able to approach situations and events with an improved attitude that will place you on a path to realize improved outcomes?
- ❖ What is your level of confidence in reviewing engagements from your past that did not go well as a learning platform to propel you to new attitudinal heights?
- ❖ How do you feel about your engagement with volunteer activities and social causes that you may support from the perspective that you are able to improve the atmosphere through positive improvements in your perspective as recognized by the attitude you display?

I trust that as you internalize your responses to the questions above you are able to tap into the super power you possess. We live our personal and professional brands daily, and the messaging we communicate begins with our attitude. Leverage and apply how you choose to define your attitude to improve situations and interactions with others in a positive manner. Our goal should be to make life better through our touchpoints.

Affirmation #11

I affirm that I will refine and protect my brand in the way I apply my positive attitude with each touchpoint as I engage with others and navigate through challenging situations.

CHAPTER **12**

A Positive Attitude and Newton's Laws of Motion

"Weakness of attitude becomes a weakness of character"
—Albert Einstein

Before you write off this chapter questioning what Sir Isaac Newton has to do with our discussion regarding attitudes, I invite you to step outside your traditional way of thinking about science. If an in-depth review of high school science or physics is not your cup of tea, you are still in a great place. No need to pull out the periodic table or engage the search engine of your choice to follow where we are about to go. On a personal level, I have always been a huge fan of science and technology, thus I could not resist the opportunity to bring in somewhat of a scientific approach to our discussion. Ideally, bringing a bit of physics is a great example to illustrate my points.

Previously I committed to taking a conversational approach toward discussing attitudes and how we have the ability to change our lives and improve our engagements with others through the attitude we choose to possess. I am holding to my commitment; however, I want to take a different approach to demonstrate the power and value of ensuring that we keep our attitude in the right place.

Sir Isaac Newton was a renowned physicist, mathematician and

scientist who lived more than 300 years ago. His scientific exploits challenged the way that many thought about science and took his field to higher level of thinking. At only twenty-three years old, Newton developed the law of universal gravitation. Although it was quite an undertaking, Newton was not quite finished doing his homework. Among his greatest accomplishments were Newton's Laws of Motion, which were developed roughly twenty years after the law of gravitation was introduced. Before I progress, and as a point of reference, here are Newton's Laws of Motion:

> "Every object persists in its state of rest or uniform motion in a straight line unless it is compelled to change that that state by forces impressed on it."
>
> "Force is equal to the change in momentum (mV) per change in time. For a constant mass, force equals mass times acceleration. F=ma"
>
> "For every action, there is an equal and opposite reaction."

Let's deal with Newton's first law of motion. In the physical world, Newton asserted that objects remain at rest and unchanged or continue traveling in an uninterrupted direction unless an external force acts on the object. In everyday language, unless something happens or if all external forces cancel each other out, an object at rest remains unchanged. If that object is already in motion, its motion does not change, and it maintains constant velocity, unless something interferes.

Think of your attitude as an object in the physical world subject to Newton's first law. Unless acted on by an outside force, your attitude either remains in a present state of rest or continues in the current state of motion unless interrupted by an outside force. The recognition of this law is essential in understanding when and where to introduce appropriate outside forces to your attitude and way of thinking. Let's go a bit further. If a person's attitude is at rest in a place of negativity and the person is consistently faced with seeing the downside of life in other people and in situations, I am willing to

bet that this is not where the person wishes to remain. For people in such a place, the recognition of this fact is the critical first step toward introducing the right positive external forces to change where their attitude resides. Once a person recognizes the familiar territory of downing others and failing to see the path to successful engagements, one can intentionally begin to introduce a new way of thinking into their daily routine. If you are serious about changing the state of *negative rest*, you must exert positivity on your attitude and move down the right path. If your attitude is already positive and in a good place, wonderful. You do not get a day off; your energy should go toward making sure that negative forces do not interrupt your state of *positive rest*. This job too is full-time. There will always be people, situations, and events happening around you with the potential to wreck your positive place. You know your world much better than I do, and I am sure you can easily assign names to people, places, and events that challenge you daily. The takeaway for you is to ensure that when your attitude is positively resting, you recognize the negative things that have the ability to move you from that place. Additionally, if your attitude is not where it needs to be, intentionally bring positive energy to the equation that can change your state of negative rest.

Newton's second law of motion introduces the concept of momentum. Using this law, Newton explained how the velocity of an object changes when that same object is exposed to an external force. He described this change as *momentum*. This force is said to be equal to momentum (mass times velocity) per a change in time. If we imagine that "m" is the mass or size of our attitude, and "a" is the acceleration of our attitude, we can reason that the force of our attitude is the product of what happens when we accelerate our attitude in a certain direction. When we apply positivity in an accelerated manner, we generate greater amounts of positive force. Conversely, when we apply negativity in an accelerated manner, we generate greater amounts of negative force. Two important questions to consider are how will you choose to define your attitude, and what forces will you use to accelerate your attitude using Newton's second law of motion?

The third law of motion from Newton asserts that for every action, there is an equal and opposite reaction. This law may be the easiest of the three laws to understand without going extremely deep into a physics discussion. When your attitude generates a force in your world, there is an equal and opposite force in existence. Does it sometimes seem that at every turn when you try hard to remain in a positive place, someone or something comes along and tries to steal your joy? We could characterize that situation as an equal and opposite force at work. Have you ever been in a place when you were not feeling or engaging with others at your best level and you kept encountering people who seemed to always display an air of positivity? If this scenario sounds familiar, it may have been an equal and opposite force at work that you witnessed. To use Newton's third law of motion to your advantage, it is essential for you to recognize two factors. The first concepts you will need to know are where you are coming from and what type of attitude you possess. Once you are aware of where your current attitude resides, you are then able to anticipate the types of equal and opposite reactions you might encounter.

As an illustration, if you know you begin the day with a negative point of view and realize you need a major dose of positivity to transform your thinking, you are in a great place to make the transformation. If that is your beginning, make it your priority to look for the equal and opposite force to your negativity as the catalyst for you to make a change. It may take only one dose of positivity to move your attitude from a place of negativity to positivity. There are days that it may take several doses of positivity to get our attitudes on the right track. As previously stated, life is tough and full of challenges. There are times that we are our own greatest challenge, which is one of the reasons why it is important that we understand the positive power we can wield, rooted in a positive attitude. If your attitude is in a positive place and you have made intentional decisions to get there, then by all means celebrate the moment. While celebrating, understand that an equal and opposite reaction may be headed your way. Once again, recognition is your ally, and you can dig your feet

in and stand your ground regardless of what person or event comes your way, knowing you will remain in a good place as far as your attitude is concerned. I am not promising you will not have a few LARGE challenges to deal with. What I am asserting is that the attitude you possess is your choice, and if you are determined to maintain your positivity when all hell is breaking loose around you, then you have overcome more than half the battle.

I want to congratulate you for keeping pace with my brief lesson in physics to illustrate my points. I am quite sure that Sir Isaac Newton did not intend his laws of motion to serve the purpose of demonstrating the dynamics of how attitudes operate. I thank Newton for influencing me to use his laws to aid your understanding. As you probably remember from school, where there is science, homework is never far behind. Your homework assignment is to think about how you can apply the laws of motion to the situations presented to you daily and understand how you either begin or continue down the path to a positive place. Here is an exercise that may help you once you find some quiet time to consider how those three laws can make a difference for you.

Attitudinal Checkup X: Guiding the Motion of My Attitude

- ❖ How does it make you feel when it seems that someone or something is trying to ruin your "positive place?" How will you handle this type of situation in the future?
- ❖ What are a few things you are able to do in advance of a challenging situation to maintain your positive attitude trajectory?
- ❖ What are a few of the red flags given off by other people that could serve as a warning to look out for an equal and opposite reaction headed your way?
- ❖ Are you able to think of a few methods to accelerate your positivity in a way that generates greater positive force in your life?

- ❖ Are you open minded and receptive enough to allow positivity to pull you from a place of negativity if you find yourself dwelling there?

It is my desire that you use the answers to the questions to keep thinking about applying the physics of a positive attitude to your everyday thinking. Make it a priority to leverage this approach and look for big results due to the choices you make.

AFFIRMATION # 12

I affirm that I will think daily about where my attitude *resides* in a state of rest and how it *moves* as a result of the forces I allow to impact my attitude.

CHAPTER **13**

Positive-Attitude-Building Exercises

As with anything that you desire to perform well, you must build your positive attitude daily.

We often marvel at what world-class athletes can achieve. In watching the Olympic Games, it is amazing to see individuals from all over the world competing at the highest levels in their respective sports. What a spectacle of excellence! What is always equally amazing is to hear of the countless hours and sweat equity these dedicated individuals invested into developing their skills and abilities. Their level of discipline, commitment, and personal sacrifice are what sets them apart from the rest of us. The process of building, developing, and maintaining a proper attitude toward life requires discipline, commitment, and sometimes personal sacrifice. Keeping a positive attitude through all that life throws at you requires a world-class effort to achieve world-class results. Are you up for the challenge? Do you visualize yourself standing on the platform of life and receiving your gold medal for your attitude? If that is your goal, it will surely take the right attitude-building exercises and regimen to get there. You see, these magnificent athletes did much more than merely think about and dream of reaching their goals. They all worked hard, trained, received great amounts of coaching, and trained their muscles to respond as needed when winning was at stake. If you are ready to get

your attitude into world-class shape, then let the games begin.

Whether you are a gold medal athlete or a novice, most will agree that proper stretching and a thorough warmup routine can make a great deal of difference and serve to avoid injuries. What a difference it makes when muscles are warm with blood flowing as an introduction as opposed to jumping in at full force. The same may be said for your attitude. Instead of jumping directly into the day or into tough situations, consider starting your daily journey with a bit of self-talk and self-coaching. If you are not quite sure what to think about or what to say out loud to yourself, begin with the affirmations presented at the conclusion of each previous chapter. Since there are more days than affirmations, use them as a starting point and then challenge yourself to write your own affirmations that are tailor-made for your life and the situations you are consistently challenged with. You may consider some of the affirmations "heavy-duty," but consider the fact that going for the gold begins in your mind. You must first think that you can achieve it and then act on that belief. Get the words of affirmation deep into your attitude, which will inform your positive thinking from the very beginning.

Once properly warmed up and ready to go, many athletes and health enthusiasts engage in core workout activities to get their heart going. There are many medical experts qualified to articulate the benefits of heart-healthy routines, and I will not attempt to steal their thunder. As I tell my daughter often, "Yes, I am a doctor, but not *that* kind of doctor!"

Many benefits have to do with becoming and remaining heart-healthy. While this type of workout impacts your physical heart, consider how a positive attitude may affect the many situations and people who are close to your heart. Think about how leveraging the power of leading with a heart-healthy attitude can make a difference through your touch points. What better way to engage your core for maximum results?

Some athletes train to achieve great proficiency with speed and agility. Can you imagine qualifying for the one-hundred-meter sprint

if it takes you three days to reach the finish line? I didn't think so. Speed, as it applies to your attitude, may involve how quickly you are able to accelerate from where you are to where you desire to reside. Remember our motion discussion from the previous chapter? Just as you can choose how your attitude will define your life, additionally you have a great deal of influence on how quickly you choose to change your attitude for the better. On the contrary, if you are able to detect that people or events are causing you to slip from your peaceful place, you may be able to slow your pace before you fall completely out of your chosen realm of positivity. There are times when we need to slow our pace of life to get our bearings. Attitude speed training will help you become an effective manager of when to slow down and when to increase your speed. At risk of invoking a cliché, life will place hurdles in your path. Similar to the track event, we sometimes get high hurdles and sometimes we get low hurdles. Regardless, a hurdle is a hurdle. Those who train relentlessly glide over each hurdle with speed and grace. This event requires speed and agility to navigate the hurdle without breaking stride. Are you adept with both speed and agility when it comes to your attitude, perhaps challenging yourself to come out of the blocks quickly when working on a project or in situations where you are interacting with others? As you approach the challenge in your lane, employ lessons learned and rely on your knowledge of how to navigate your hurdle and soar above it. Call on your positive history to know how to lift yourself over the bar and how to land safely on the ground without breaking your stride. Life can sometimes seem like a perpetual hurdle challenge with no end in sight. We must train and prepare ourselves to cross each hurdle with the heart of a winner, knowing that each one we successfully navigate with winning speed and with a winning level of agility gets us closer to the finish line. A track meet has many different events. Once you clear your immediate hurdles, catch your breath and get ready for your next event.

Sometimes, other athletes employ many of the same routines that track and field athletes use to excel. I am convinced that countless

lessons from life can be taught using sports and athletics, which is one of the reasons why engaging in sports can be such a positive endeavor for young children and adults. Besides promoting a healthy lifestyle, there is much to learn.

Strength training enables us to build a strong muscular base, supports our frame, and permits us to move our bodies as required to complete all that we seek to do daily. There are quite a few approaches to strength training to choose from. Essentially, building muscle involves challenging your muscles to do more through increased resistance or through repetitive exercises or motions that increase flexibility and result in bigger, stronger muscles. Shifting our thoughts back to our attitude, consider how engaging in situations with greater challenges prepares us to take on larger and more challenging situations with greater ease. With strength training, starting with lighter weights and reps is usually a better start, as opposed to attempting to begin on the upper end of the weight rack or thinking you will max out repetitions immediately. In building your attitude muscles, begin by navigating some of your lesser challenges prior to jumping into the most challenging ones first. If you know that conversations with a particular person has not been favorable in the past, change your strategy. Explore what I will call meaningful small talk, and when possible, look for commonalities between you and the other person instead of starting with the most contentious topics and conversations you can think of. **Be sure to get this fact, regardless of whether you begin with a person or begin with a challenging situation: your attitude is your starting point!** From where your attitude currently resides, leverage your experience to build up to the large weights in building your attitudinal muscles.

In developing a world-class attitude there are other factors to incorporate into your training regimen. Serious athletes are often disciplined when it comes to their diet. Some go to extreme measures to monitor and control what they consume. This level of discipline is beneficial in supporting the overall goal of getting into shape and maintaining an optimal level of physical conditioning. When it

comes to your attitude, it is necessary to develop a sense of discipline and monitor what influences your attitude. There is a visual and healthy difference between individuals who consistently consume high-quality and healthy foods and beverages in comparison to those who either choose not to consume healthy food or are limited in their ability to access healthy options. While we are constantly bombarded with myriad situations and individuals from diverse backgrounds and experiences, we must serve as the gatekeeper of how these people and events affect us by informing our attitude. In our attitudinal conditioning, do we allow the slightest things over which we have no control to take our attitude to a place where it does not belong? Do we approach people with positivity and confidence by leveraging the experience of what was successful in the past?

Managing discipline around your attitudinal diet requires sacrifice, just as managing your physical diet does. Perhaps you are tempted by overindulging in starches, or maybe you enjoy sugar-based soft drinks more than you should. Sacrifice may mean walking away from the drink machine on the job or drinking water, with lemon if you prefer, with your meal. Sacrifice may take the form of multiple servings of fresh vegetables on your plate with fewer servings of breads and starches. Your attitudinal diet may require you to walk away from certain situations. You may need to carefully consider whom you interact with when possible, if that person is toxic to your level of positivity. We may not always have the ability to remove ourselves from every situation; however, do not despair. Think back to our previous discussion about events and people we cannot control. A healthy diet of what we consume is essential, whether we are talking about physical food or the things that we internalize that influence our attitude. In both instances, you are what you eat. Be sure to maintain a healthy diet.

When talking about world-class athletes and world-class attitudes there is one practice I cannot leave out of the discussion. Many successful athletes engage in a high level of visualization while training as preparation for the moment when they must perform in

competition. Successful baseball pitchers see themselves executing the desired wind up and delivery of the ball long before they approach the mound during a game. Before the race begins, sprinters see themselves breaking away from the pack at the right time to claim first place. Golfers envision making the long putt many times before they are under the pressure to perform. Successful outcomes are the result of many things. Practice, conditioning, diet, a proper warmup, sweat, resilience, and coaching are all vital. At some point, one must put all of the component parts together and visualize what success looks like. This is an opportunity for your attitude to make you or break you. Does your attitude position you to think that you will have successful interactions with others? Are you seeing positivity in challenging situations, or are you the first one to exit the "room of positivity" when the slightest element of opposition shows up? If you are a believer in the notion that success breeds success, then your key to successful (positive) interactions may be birthed from the visualization of positivity, starting with your attitude.

Sometimes what we concentrate on becomes a self-fulfilling prophecy. If you believe this to be true, why would you fail to focus on positivity and positive outcomes as opposed to maintaining your focus on adverse performance and potentially less than successful outcomes?

We have reached another check point to consider where we are relative to our exercise routines for success. Let's go!

Attitudinal Checkup XI: Training and Preparation

- ❖ How do you feel about your ability to successfully employ a level of attitudinal agility that enables you to work through unforeseen challenges?
- ❖ What strength-building practices do you employ that result in an enhanced level of positivity and allow you to move through challenges with greater ease?
- ❖ How do you feel about strengthening your core in order to take care of the priorities and people close to your heart? If

you are not up for the challenge, what needs to happen to prepare you to do so?

- How do you feel about what you spend your time visualizing?
- How would you rate your attitudinal diet, and what are some of the major temptations that prevent you from a level of healthy consumption required to fuel yourself with positivity?
- Name a few positive practices and routines that will accelerate your progress to the attitudinal finish line or the winner's circle reserved only for those with world-class attitudes?

Developing a world-class attitude filled with positivity is challenging to say the least. Just to let you know that I do not live in some fantasy land, I too must deal with all that I am encouraging you to do in this chapter and in this book. The reality is that life can be brutal and unforgiving. People sometimes get in the way and inhibit our ability to remain positive. Situations and events place hurdles in our path. We must constantly train ourselves and prepare for the hurdles in order to endure the race. We must do our best to ready ourselves through active strength building, healthy routines, and a great attitudinal diet. World-class athletes spend a great deal of time developing their bodies getting their muscles ready for competition. I am confident that if you are **serious** about getting positivity into your DNA, you will seriously work hard to make it happen through your routines and through your regimen. Even the most developed muscles will atrophy if they are not regularly used and challenged to deliver optimal performance. Do not put in the work to develop a great attitude filled with positivity only to render it valueless by placing it on your inner shelf. How will you ever impact the world in a positive way if you follow that route? Along the way, make time for proper rest and refueling. We are not machines; thus, we require healthy downtime. Even during your downtime, consider meditating on thoughts and concepts that can influence your attitude in a positive way. As you define your attitude and make choices that support the development positivity, always consider and focus on your personal winner's circle

and visualize standing tall on the podium of life wearing **Attitude Gold!**

AFFIRMATION #13

I affirm that I will intentionally and consistently engage in positive attitude-building activities that will develop and maintain my world-class positive attitude.

CHAPTER **14**

Putting It All Together

Achieving a world-class positive attitude requires commitment, dedication, training, and a lot of practice. Get started today.

Congratulations, my friend! You are almost through this volume, and I applaud you for your resilience. Although you are approaching the end of this book, I trust you view it as the beginning of a new chapter in your life. Together we have covered a lot of ground and explored many different elements toward understanding attitudes and how to claim your world-class positive attitude. Your toolbox should now be well equipped with a few specialized items to help you master your attitude and use your attitude to drive the outcomes and consequences you desire in your life. Your challenge now is to put it all together and formulate your game plan of how to navigate your journey using this information. This book is your recipe for success, and any good recipe is composed of required ingredients and directions for assembly. Up to this point, the discussion has allowed you to assemble the parts and complete required preparations. Now we are ready to put it all together for the masterpiece we wish to create.

Your willingness to understand more about how attitudes can operate for your benefit or how they can surely sink you is the first step toward making progress. Your level of willingness and ability to take advantage of the concepts presented can make a monumental

difference in your life. **Life is too short for any of us to waste time possessing an adverse attitude and a low expectation of what we can achieve.** Depending on your starting point, you may have a great deal of road to travel to realize what I will call effective attitude management (EAM). After reading this book, you may realize you are a lot closer to where you wish to be based on leveraging previous successes. One notion for certain is that regardless of our starting point, each of us can improve and incorporate a more positive approach to life beginning with the attitude that we choose to possess.

Why bother? I trust that I've done a sufficient job of convincing you that you are an extremely valuable person and the world needs you to develop and maintain a positive attitude and approach to life. Your family needs you to exist at your best and deserves you at your best with a positive attitude. Consider your touch points and the impact of your touch as discussed in previous chapters. There are countless opportunities for each of us to make a difference through the people we engage with and through the initiatives that we support. I challenge you not to let an adverse attitude take you or your dreams hostage. Take control of your attitude and develop a lifestyle of positivity. I still hear a few naysayers in the shadows who believe this is some dreamy-happy story that will never work for them. I will be the first to say that this message may NOT resonate with everyone. This message should resonate with those who are serious about moving forward in life in a more positive way, regardless of whom you encounter, regardless of your challenges, regardless of the circumstances that always seem to happen to you, and regardless of your history. If you do not wish to make a positive impact on this world or if you do not care about how others define you, then my message may not ring any bells with you. I am willing to bet there are individuals in your life you would like to see make a commitment to improve by gaining a world-class positive attitude. If you never encounter those individuals, then you are truly in a great place.

Putting it all together begins with your beliefs. If you believe you can do better, you can. If you believe you are able to deal with less

than positive situations without undue stress and worry, you can. If you believe you are able to create positive outcomes when it seems there is nothing positive about your current situation, then yes, you can. Perhaps it is a matter of simple human nature, if you believe *simple human nature* is not an oxymoron. We tend to gravitate toward the things we believe. While that statement is not necessarily a profound one, the same notion in many instances reveals the life path some individuals traverse daily. Once you believe, then you are able to move forward and infuse positivity in all that you touch or influence.

Notice that action must follow your belief. While belief is necessary as a state of mind, *action* is what gets it done. My desire is that you **take action** based on what you have discovered through our dialogue. As previously stated, life is tough, challenging, difficult, and full of twists and turns. Some are great or fantastic; others, not so much. The belief that you are able to live positively and make a positive difference begins within you.

Putting it all together involves being an excellent *gatekeeper* of what "*gets*" to you. Let's be real, some people and some situations get under our skin and drive us nuts. We do not live inside a bubble; neither are we able to avoid all interaction with others. What things get you moving in a positive direction or in a negative direction? Putting it together involves equipping yourself to deal with either in your best way possible. Pay close attention here. I stated that you are equipping yourself to deal with life in your best way possible. I am neither clairvoyant nor able to look into some magical crystal ball and provide you with all that you will ever need to continue your journey. Ideally, I am able to create valuable, relevant conversations that enable you to develop your personalized success plan. After all, I cannot claim to know you better than you know yourself. Use my words and notions as guidance to achieve the type of attitude that you long to possess.

Think once again about the progression of our model and how we navigate from the first to the last stage.

The Infinity Attitude Cycle

One does not arrive at consequences without moving through the previous stages. Additionally, each stage builds on the prior level. As we now know, it all begins with our attitude. Thoughts, actions, outcomes, and consequences track back to the type of attitude that we begin with. There is a direct relationship from our point of origin to our resulting consequences. Although I have walked you through this information previously, I wanted to revisit this important relationship to provide context for an extremely important point. Be sure to get this point deep into your mind as a part of challenging yourself to go further:

Do not allow a good attitude to prevent you from pursuing a great attitude!

Depending on your starting point, achieving a good attitude may be quite a stretch. Do all that is within your power to achieve a good attitude as your "opening act." Celebrate the moment and reflect on what got you there, for you have done a good thing. For some, a good attitude may be all you desire. Many have the capacity to develop a world-class positive attitude, yet lack the desire to get there. If you are such a person, I encourage you to make the most of your good attitude. Make sure you consistently display a good attitude in all that you do. Many good people are doing good things in a good way all around us. Good is important. Let's not take it for granted.

My primary point to stress here is that good(ness) has the potential to prevent you from achieving great(ness). Let's revisit the analogy of world-class athletes, scholars, performers, or people who have separated themselves from the majority of others inhabiting the earth. At the time of this writing, a person would have to be extremely knowledgeable to recite the names of the top twenty-five sprinters in the world in the hundred-meter event. I will argue that if you are in this

elite group, you are not only good, you are very good at this event. Among those considered very good, a few names continue to lead the way as world-class. Who can think of this track and field event without the name Usaine Bolt coming to mind? His dominance of this event not only established him as the best in the world, it also took the status of world-class in this event to another level. When others name individuals who consistently display a good attitude, is your name among them? If you are not there today, are you committed to getting there? If your name is already on the list of those possessing a good attitude, are you working to achieve world-class attitude status? Are you aware of what it will take to elevate your game to the next level and beyond?

There is another world-class professional I wish to highlight in this chapter. His name is Dr. Kenston J. Griffin, founder and CEO of Dream Builders Communication, Inc. Dr. Griffin is a phenomenal CEO, keynote speaker, author, and mentor. One of his signature quotes aligns perfectly with this section, and I will share it with you here:

"If better is possible, good is no longer an option!"
—Dr. Kenston J. Griffin

The first few times I heard this statement and read it, I accepted it at face value; however, I have learned to adopt this statement as life-changing for me. As well as I know myself, there are areas where I've been able to identify opportunities to get better and improve. As I listened to honest feedback from trusted sources, others have identified opportunities for me to realize that better is possible. Once that realization settled into my spirit, it became mission critical for me to figure out how to improve from good to something better. With all the thoughts, I had about developing a positive attitude, of course I had to internalize this same approach and consider ways to improve the level of positivity in my own attitude. It became glaringly clear to me that better was indeed possible, thus good was no longer an acceptable option. I challenge you to do the same. You know where you are right now, and I

am trusting that after a bit of self-inspection and self-discovery, you will learn of a few areas that will improve the level of positivity in your attitude. If you truly believe that a better attitude is possible, then you do yourself a disservice to settle on a good attitude.

When it comes to your attitude, always consider the amazing responsibility you have to manage it appropriately. What an asset you have, if you are defined by a world-class positive attitude. What a liability you have if you are defined by a negative or adverse attitude. Either way, it is yours. In a previous paragraph, we reached a celebration point for good attitudes. I do not want you to get comfortable with a good attitude. The world needs more world-class positive attitudes. For a moment consider any area of your life or discipline of your choosing. Your choice could be your government, your job, the community organization where you volunteer your time, your church, your social club, or just the group of individuals you regularly spend time with. We know we are met with challenges on all fronts, even in the places where we make a conscientious choice to spend time among people we've chosen to be around. Regardless of your situation, I do not want you to dwell on those thoughts for too long. Now consider those same relationships, except this time I want to you to consider what life would look like for you if the majority of those you interact with possessed world-class positive attitudes. If the majority of those you interact with have already mastered this high level of positivity, then great for you.

Let's make it a bit more personal. Imagine how much you could make a greater positive impact and what life would look like for others, once you too possess a world-class positive attitude, if you are not already there. If you are not quite there yet, I congratulate you for the progress you have already made. If you have reached "good," then good for you. Now let's go to "great" and not let good stand in our way. The last time I checked, great was better than good. And "If better is possible, then good is no longer an option!" The world needs you at great! Your family needs you at great! The organizations and jobs where you spend great amounts of time will be better off once

you achieve a great world-class level of positivity.

How many times have we heard stories of individuals who in their later years sat down and reflected on all they achieved as they grew up, matured, and reached what they defined as their peak prior to settling into their senior years? It is wonderful to hear of individuals' personal accounts of the things they did, what they accomplished, and how they navigated the road called life. There is oftentimes a certain wisdom conveyed through the stories and recounts of their journeys. I have heard many such stories and often walk away in amazement, knowing what took place in the lives of others. In the words of these individuals, they have told me that they lived and continued to live a good life. Individuals have responded that if they had to do it over again, they would have made different decisions. In some instances, I've been bold enough to ask what would have made the difference in some of the decisions that they made. Get ready for this. I have been told that a *difference in attitude* and a difference in their perspective on life would have made a great difference in the choices they made.

Little did I know at the time that this sort of feedback would feed into a chapter of this book. I could not have known in a million years. I do recognize the power of the message of what was conveyed to me. First, there is power in the ability to reflect on paths previously traveled as a means of determining future successes. Sometimes the learning curve may be long or steep; however, if we pay close attention we may walk away from people and situations armed for future success. My lesson learned is that a dose of healthy self-reflection is a valuable tool to employ as a critical data point for future decisions and future successes.

My second observation from these discussions revealed to me that we do not have to live on the edge, thinking every decision we make is mission critical. Some decisions formed by our attitudes have lesser value and impact than others. We are not perfect, thus our particular attitude toward life at any given moment will not be perfect. Additionally, even when individuals spoke to the fact that a different attitude toward life would have likely yielded different results, they

still had, in their own opinions, a good life.

My third observation came from listening to what sounded less like regrets from the past and more of feelings of wonder, when considering what could have been, had an attitude or approach to life been different. Those responses really resonated with my thoughts of how much a positive approach and a positive perspective have the ability to make a difference. This was revealing to me. As I engaged individuals across diverse age ranges, I had very similar types of conversations. I wanted to understand whether individuals saw attitude as an essential driver of their success in life. I continue to initiate these conversations, and thus far, an overwhelming majority of people I've spoken with see and value their ability to positively affect their successful navigation through life using the lens of a positive attitude.

Putting it all together involves making this information understandable and usable on a daily basis. While this book may conjure a few interesting conversations and discussion topics, my desire is to positively change lives by helping individuals apply this information in their daily routines and through their life journey. You could have invested your time reading and reviewing plenty of other things. There are many other topics I am sure represent items and areas of great value to you. It is my desire that by now this information has moved into your grouping of **"top value"** items in your life. Putting it all together to effectively gain and maintain a world-class positive attitude is worth the effort.

It is time for more introspective thinking. I present you with the following questions to consider that may help you to bring it all together for your benefit.

When military units prepare to launch a mission, they employ all sorts of questionnaires and checks to ensure mission readiness. Corporate organizations do the same to ensure that optimal levels of readiness are achieved prior to launching projects and initiatives. I want you to ensure that you are ready to pull it all together as you kick off your mission to achieve or maintain your world-class positive attitude.

Attitudinal Checkup XII: Readiness for Mission Deployment

- How do you now feel about your level of readiness to engage in positive attitude-building routines that will support a world-class attitude daily?
- When considering a few of your own life experiences, how do you feel about your ability to recognize when you are exhibiting a world-class positive attitude? Do you recognize when you have more work to do to get there?
- Take out a sheet of paper and capture what a good attitude looks like for you, and then capture what you believe a world-class positive attitude looks like for your life. Place your response in a safe place. Be sure to remember where you place it, and pull it out once a month as a reminder of where you are and where you are going, and remember we tend to gravitate toward the things that we think about regularly (both positive and negative).
- Find three people you trust to provide you with honest, healthy feedback related to the attitude you possess. Have them document their responses as follows: provide three positive words or short phrases to describe your attitude, and three words of opportunity or areas of improvement regarding your attitude. **You are not looking for a drawn-out discussion extended debate. Your job is not to explain or rationalize why you are the way that you are. What is important for you to understand is how individuals you trust have defined you based on your attitude. (Be sure to complete this task prior to taking on the next one.)**
- Now that you have a few data points from your personal introspection and others' observations, how do you feel about your ability to achieve the world-class positive attitude that is waiting for you?

This Attitudinal Checkup was slightly different, since I asked you to get outside of your own head for what I trust was valuable feedback. Ideally, we are able to align what we strive to achieve with how others view and define us. Remember, we cannot control others, which is not our goal. At the same time, if I am only great in my own head, in opposition with the rest of the world, then what have I really accomplished? Do your best to bring this information together for your long-term success toward reaching your attitudinal goals and milestones, and do not get comfortable with good successes. Go for the gold! Putting it all together and using the tools will ensure that you do not create a story similar to the talented homebuilder from a previous chapter who had all of the right tools and choose not to use them.

Affirmation #14

I affirm that I will always strive for a great, positive, world-class attitude and not be satisfied with achieving a good attitude.

CHAPTER **15**

Write Your Story

When building your life legacy, make sure your positive attitude is a main character in your story.

As you are about to wrap up reading *Defined by Attitude*, you are at a very important stage of your existence. The reflection you now face is what to do with all of the information you have received or gleaned from your introspective thoughts. I want to switch roles with you now. No, I cannot become you, and you cannot become me. Up to this point, I have been the author and you have been my gracious audience. I am ready for you to take the role of author for a bit. Imagine your life as an open book, an unfinished book. Many chapters have already been written. They are in ink, or for those not old enough to remember writing with ink, imagine those chapters are on a non-erasable hard drive or somewhere in "the cloud" and forever memorialized. The great opportunity in front of you is to write the remainder of **your story** based on what you now know. Revisiting an earlier point, begin the remainder of your story with the end in mind and with your attitude as the foundation. How do you desire your next chapters to read? What impact do you wish to make, and how do you wish to make it? Will others remember you as the one who always approached life with a fresh perspective and one who always maintained a productive, world-class positive attitude? Will you

be the one who too often saw only the negative and cringed when a golden opportunity was disguised as a bit of hard work?

I proudly developed and wrote what you have been reading with the goal of helping others. I want to inspire you to reach the Attitude Hall of Fame. Even if no such place exists today, I want to have you ready for induction the minute the doors open. I now challenge you to proudly write the next chapters of your life with the proper orientation around attitude as your feather and quill. I know, I went beyond *old-school* with that reference, but I trust you get my point. You are neither hopeless nor a hapless victim of random happenings. Think about what you can control then write your story.

I can imagine a few individuals saying, "I've never written a story and certainly never an autobiography." Do not worry; you are the subject and the center of attention. This is your opportunity to be the star of the show. What I am asking you to accomplish will carry you further than having your name in the center of a star on the Hollywood Walk of Fame. There are many stars with their names permanently etched there, and I salute them for achieving such a high level of fame and recognition for their career achievements. This is your opportunity to achieve legendary status in your story with your attitude. You actually have several roles. You are the author, director, star, critic, and historian. I trust you are up to the task and ready to go to begin.

Writing your own story involves several important decisions you will need to make. Among them, you will need to evaluate and consider where you are right now in respect to your attitude. Are you in a good place, and are you willing to go from good to world-class? This single decision has the ability to affect much of what you will commit to doing. I challenge you to spend a bit of concentrated time thinking about your current state. If you do not know where to begin, pray for guidance and meditate on what you know about yourself. Make a list and take an inventory of your attitudinal assets and liabilities. Once you see it on paper, you may have better insight in terms of where you want or need to take your attitude to reach your next level of

greatness. Remember an early point from chapter one. The best maps in the world cannot help you if you are not keenly aware of your starting point. Take the time to thoroughly know where you are beginning your journey, to write the remainder of your story.

Writing the remainder of your story may require you to step out with faith and bold confidence that you are more than capable and able to tackle all that life has in store for you, even if you have never done it before. Where is your faith, and what do you believe you are able to accomplish? We tend to value where our beliefs reside. Where do your beliefs lie?

My friend, none of us possess that elusive crystal ball to tell us what the remainder of our story will look like. Even if we knew, how exciting would life be if we already knew every twist and turn ahead and in our path? Yes, it would be fun to know a few things in advance; however, life does not always turn out that way. What you are able to do is make the commitment that beginning today you are on **your** path toward attitudinal greatness. Intimate knowledge of your path is essential. Do not get caught up attempting to move through a life path never intended for you to travel. At risk of sounding redundant, I will state this important bit of guidance again, because I want to make sure you really get this one: **Do not get caught up attempting to move through a life path never intended for you to travel.**

Realizing where you are and where you want to go is critical to understanding what path is for you. Regardless of your age, who wants to wake up one morning ten years from now realizing that the primary source of your unending frustration is because of trying to navigate a path never created for you? I certainly do not! Writing your life story involves a heavy dose of knowing yourself.

Numerous experts can articulate in great depth all the required elements of a great story. I will not attempt to write a thesis recapturing those well-documented points. I will take some time to touch on a few commonly mentioned elements to provide you with a framework to begin writing your story. By now you must know that you are the main character. No further explanation required. A great story often

involves a plot, defined as the conflict or challenge the main character works through. Your challenge is developing your world-class attitude and using it to navigate through all that life is serving up for you. Although I do not know your personal stories or the path of your life, I am willing to bet there are some prime-time accounts of life out there. Your plot alone may be enough to create a top-grossing movie and accompanying sequels. In knowing your plot, be sure you are writing and working from your script and not a script belonging to someone else. Imagine you prepare to audition for a role as a deep-sea commercial fisherman. You complete great amounts of research and study the life of fishermen. On the day of your audition, you arrive and are asked to read and play the part of a deep-space engineer, when you know nothing about this role. What happened? You studied the wrong script! The same can happen in your life if you are operating from the wrong script.

Many will agree that great stories involve a hero or heroine, someone who saves the day and sets everything right in the world. This is your opportunity to create the script that will enable you to be the attitude hero in your story as the main character. You can neither predict nor control your future. What you can control is how you choose to react to the myriad events that will happen to you over the course of your life. We know you cannot control the individuals who will cross your path. We know that our inability to control others no longer causes us any undue stress. With the burden of control removed from your plate, you are free to concentrate on being the hero or heroine. Are you ready to live up to this status?

Just as there is a hero, a great story involves a villain. I will help you identify your villain. As opposed to naming a person who may challenge you in your current situation, we will name something far worthier of the title of your true villain. **The villain in your story is a negative attitude.** Tell me you saw that one coming! That is correct, the dragon that ould slay you is an attitude filled with negativity. As you write your story, be sure to incorporate all the tools, weapons, and tactics required to take down the dragon of a negative attitude. If

metaphorical dragons are too far-fetched for you to visualize, imagine a negative attitude as a futuristic being from the deep realms of outer space sent here to adversely affect all that you do from this day forward. Certainly, you would not stand by passively and watch it happen. I would expect you to battle to achieve all of the good that was destined for you. In writing your story, prepare to battle to achieve the world-class attitude you need for life-changing success.

The last element of a great story is the setting. Simply, this is where your story takes place. We live action-packed lives with information traveling globally in nanoseconds. Advances in technology have made travel more affordable and more convenient than previously experienced. We are able to change our setting quickly and continuously. Within your story, your setting is wherever you are and wherever you are represented. If you spend a great deal of time in the social media atmosphere, that world too is a part of your setting, at least in a virtual sense. For some individuals, social media interaction and minute-by-minute postings of every single activity they engage in is real-time. Live streaming has removed the wait-and-see factor from much of what individuals experience daily and expands your setting. As I share with my maturing daughter, once you send the e-mail, post your message, or otherwise communicate by any of the various social media choices, it cannot be taken back. We see countless stories of individuals who post thoughts in a moment of rage, only to regret it later. You may take down the post; however, you have no idea who saw it or how many times it was shared with others before you took it down. I too enjoy the conveniences and capabilities offered by today's technology. I recognize that by way of my smartphone, my setting is now global. Be sure to keep this setting in mind when writing your story.

Time for your final checkup in this volume.

Attitudinal Checkup XIII: Writing Your Story

- ❖ How do you feel about your ability to assess where you are in order to create a script for your world-class attitude based on what you know?
- ❖ How do you feel about known hurdles that have the potential to challenge your ability to be the hero or heroine that you desire to be?
- ❖ Since life does not happen in a linear fashion, how would you rate your ability to navigate through multiple and random events and people who may challenge your ability to live the script you will write?
- ❖ As a follow-up to the previous question, describe your willingness to go "off script" when necessary to adjust to unforeseen challenges.

This chapter was written to help you see the importance of developing what I referred to as your script. Essentially your script is your plan to achieve the life you desire through the attitude you choose. Pay attention to the last two questions from above and know there will be occasions that may challenge you to edit your script when necessary, to overcome an immediate situation. Do not consider yourself a failure if you must take that course of action. Once the immediate challenge is handled, make it your business to take one of two courses of action. One action is to become reengaged with your script to maintain your forward momentum and achieve your goal of a world-class attitude. Setbacks and unforeseen things will occur. It is essential not to get permanently sidetracked by a temporary setback.

The second option may require you to revisit your script. Experience is a great teacher, and while I encourage and admire resiliency, we sometimes reach a point in the journey that may require a new path to our destination. Recognize this fact and know that you are not a failure should you reach that point. Be reasonable. You probably will never make material progress if your script changes

every week. Give yourself time to familiarize yourself with your script and take the time to incorporate it into your daily life. You do remember there are no days off when it comes to developing and leveraging a positive attitude. I believe in you and trust that you will write your story well and in a way that enables you to claim world-class status. Write your story, and I will look to see you in the winner's circle wearing gold!

AFFIRMATION #15

I affirm that I will create the story that I want others to know me by, based on the world-class attitude I will develop and use at all times.

Parting Words

Armed with positivity, become an agent of positive change.

As the author of *Defined by Attitude*, I thank you for taking the time to read this book, which is the first in The Attitude Series! I am excited to share my thoughts with you and look forward to beginning book two. I hope my writing has caused you to think deeper about the life-changing power embedded in our attitudes. We define ourselves by the attitude we choose, and others do the same. What we choose, we own 100%, along with every consequence we encounter as the result of our choice.

While it is my desire that you have enjoyed reading this book, I wanted to go much further than present you with another entertainment option. My goal is to change lives by helping individuals understand the power of a positive attitude and assist my audience with understanding how to apply the awesome power of positivity in every aspect of life. For those who are committed to exploring how they view attitudes with the goal of developing a world-class positive attitude, I believe that my writing will resonate with you.

Completing this book has been quite a journey, and I thank the many people who offered feedback and challenged my thinking along the way. I ask that you internalize this information and use it to claim the positive attitude you are capable of possessing. In parting, consider the various ways you are now armed to improve lives, organizations, jobs, and relationships by embracing or continuing a

life full of attitudinal positivity.

We are parting for now; however, I look forward to continuing this important conversation with you. In the meantime, reach out and share your thoughts and perspectives with me. Feel free to share details of your journey or send your comments and observations via email to **info@infinityleadershipconsulting.org**, subject line: DBA-My Journey. I wish you well on your journey. Remember the words of my coach, **"If better is possible, then good is no longer an option!"** I encourage you to apply that same rationale to your attitude and establish your world-class positive attitude beginning today. Employ **Effective Attitude Management** for a better life and use your world-class positive attitude as your lens for life.

Acknowledgments and Dedication

I owe a debt of gratitude to many individuals who have been with me and supported my vision to bring this writing to fruition. Completing such an endeavor would not have been possible without family, and I have many family members to acknowledge and thank. I thank my lovely wife, Tracy, and our beautiful daughter, Kamdyn, for your support and for being a huge inspiration and motivation for me always. When I see the two of you, I know that all of the late nights in front of my laptop were worth it. Kamdyn, rest assured that I included you in my book. I thank my father, the late Mr. Robert L. Morton, Sr., and my mother, Mrs. Dorothy Morton for instilling in me a desire to dream bigger and encouraging me to find my place in life. I am still dreaming, and though the search continues, I know I am several steps closer to walking in my purpose that my Heavenly Father created uniquely for me. I thank my siblings, cousins, nieces, nephews, and the many members of my extended family, including those who have already left this earth.

I acknowledge and thank my YBM and YBW Leadership Alliance Family, my Keeneland Family, and my ITSMF Family. I owe a special debt of appreciation to "The Mighty 33," my ITSMF Management Associate cohorts who remind me *daily* of what Family is all about. I am thankful to my "Mountain Top" Family and to my close friends and colleagues who supported me and provided valuable feedback along the way. I appreciate you for helping get this vision out of my head and into my manuscript. I thank my Book Launch Team

also walk-the-walk. Dr. Morton passionately believes in the power of positivity and that our positive attitude is essential to achieve any level of life success and fulfillment.

Defined by Attitude: The Power of Positivity will lift each of us to aim higher, enhance the quality of our lives and create a greater number of positive outcomes through our touchpoints. If you, your company, your non-profit organization or your leadership team are serious about taking a leap into a greater realm of personal positivity, this book was written for you. Allow Dr. Kenneth Morton to serve as your personal Positivity Coach!

Dr. Kenston J. Griffin
CEO; Dream Builders Communication, Inc.
www.dreambuilderscommunication.com

Foreword

The manner in which we live our lives and the ways that we approach people and situations has a profound impact upon the quality of our existence. Many individuals regularly "get it right" while others consistently miss the mark. A common thread which guides either success or failure to achieving a quality existence is undoubtedly one's attitude. ***Defined by Attitude: The Power of Positivity*** is an important exploration of attitudes and may yield a life changing positive transformation for each of us.

Many struggle to "keep it real" and remain positive through all that life brings them on a daily basis. For those who are challenged by situations involving others or with life-events, Dr. Morton provides insight and a pathway to help us navigate through these rough waters. For those who already operate with positivity, he provides a path to achieve a world-class positive attitude. Within the book, each reader will discover a step-by-step approach to refine and improve their level of positivity.

This work came about from Dr. Morton's diverse life experiences and from serving in leadership roles in three Fortune 500 companies. His perspectives presented are not intended as a quick path to an attitude fix. This work is a message of how to develop, embrace and sustain a life of positivity beginning today regardless of your starting point. I realize that this message is not just what he captured in so many pages, it is an affirmation of his lens for life and the level of positivity that he embraces daily. In order to talk-the-talk you must

Table of Contents

Defined by Attitude
The Power of Positivity

v4.0

Outskirts Press, Inc.
http://www.outskirtspress.com

Paperback ISBN: 978-1-4787-9012-9

PRINTED IN THE UNITED STATES OF AMERICA

DR. KENNETH

DEFINED *by* ATTITUDE

THE POWER OF POSITIVITY

Sis. Deborah,

May God Continue to bless you in a Positive Way!

outskirts press

George realizes the importance of focusing on what he wants to achieve rather than dwelling on negative circumstances. He learns to shift his focus from problems to solutions and from complaints to gratitude.

Chapter 11 - The Power of Positive Energy:
George witnesses the transformative power of positive energy as his team starts to work together more effectively and achieve better results. He understands that positive energy can truly fuel success.

Chapter 12 - George Takes a Walk:
In an effort to continue his personal growth, George takes a walk to reflect on his journey and reinforce his commitment to positive energy. He takes time to appreciate the beauty around him and finds inspiration.

Chapter 13 - One Great Golf Shot Theory:
George learns a valuable lesson from a golf pro about focusing on the present moment and giving his best effort in every situation. He realizes that every action, no matter how small, contributes to his overall success.

Chapter 14 - Bus Tickets:
George starts giving away "bus tickets" to people who inspire and uplift him. These tickets serve as a symbol

of appreciation and recognition for their positive energy.

Chapter 15 - A Very Long Weekend:
George decides to take a weekend trip with his family to recharge and reconnect. He embraces the opportunity to spend quality time with his loved ones and create positive memories.

Chapter 16 - Who's on the Bus:
George reflects on the people he surrounds himself with and realizes that it's important to have positive, supportive individuals on his bus. He understands the influence that others can have on his energy and success.

Chapter 17 - The Enemy Is Negativity:
George becomes aware of the destructive power of negativity and its ability to derail his progress. He learns to identify negative thoughts and emotions and replaces them with positive ones.

Chapter 18 - No Energy Vampires on the Bus:
George decides to remove energy vampires from his life – people who drain his positive energy and bring him down. He focuses on surrounding himself with individuals who uplift and inspire him.

Chapter 19 - The Ultimate Rule of Positive Energy:

George discovers the ultimate rule of positive energy: love. He realizes that love is the most powerful and positive force, capable of transforming his life and the lives of those around him.

Chapter 20 - George Takes Control of His Bus:
George fully embraces his role as the driver of his own bus and takes control of his life and energy. He commits to living with purpose, passion, and positivity.

Chapter 21 - George Has a Dream:
George experiences a vivid dream that reaffirms his commitment to positive energy and inspires him to share his message with a larger audience. He realizes that he has the power to make a positive impact on the world.

Chapter 22 - Better Today than Yesterday:
In the final chapter, George reflects on his journey and the positive changes he has made. He understands that every day presents an opportunity to be better than the day before and continues to fuel his life, work, and team with positive energy.

Chapter 1 - Flat Tire

Key Lessons

1. Embrace Challenges: Life is full of unexpected challenges, like a flat tire. Instead of being frustrated and resentful, try to see them as opportunities for growth and learning. Every problem has a gift hidden within it.

2. Choose Your Perspective: Your attitude and perspective shape your experiences. You can choose to see a flat tire as a curse or an inconvenience, or you can choose to see it as a chance to learn, adapt, and find a solution. Your perspective determines whether your life is a success story or a soap opera.

3. Be Open to Help: Sometimes, when faced with difficulties, we tend to close ourselves off from receiving help. It's important to be open and willing to accept assistance from others. Recognize that asking for help doesn't make you weak or less capable; it's a sign of strength and an opportunity to connect with others.

Self-reflection Questions

1. How can you shift your perspective when faced with unexpected challenges to see them as opportunities for growth and learning?

2. Are you open to receiving help and support from others when faced with difficulties, or do you tend to close yourself off? How can you cultivate a mindset of openness and willingness to accept assistance?

Chapter 2 - Good News and Bad News

Key Lessons

1. The Power of Perspective: George's experience with the flat tire and the mechanic's news highlights the importance of seeing both the good and bad in a situation. By shifting his perspective, George could appreciate the good news of avoiding a potential accident and being grateful for his safety.

2. The Value of Awareness: George's disregard for the notice from the car manufacturer serves as a reminder to be aware of important information and not dismiss it without consideration. Being attentive and responsive to notifications can prevent future inconveniences or even potential dangers.

3. Embrace Unexpected Opportunities: Instead of dwelling on the inconvenience of leaving his car in the shop, George could have recognized the unexpected opportunity for personal growth, reflection, or exploring alternative means of transportation. Embracing unforeseen circumstances with a positive mindset opens doors to new experiences and perspectives.

Self-reflection Questions

1. How can you choose to see challenges as opportunities for growth and learning in your own life?

2. Are you open to accepting help and support from others when faced with difficulties, or do you tend to shut yourself off? How can you cultivate a mindset of openness and willingness to receive assistance?

Chapter 3 - The Long Walk Home

Key Lessons

1. Embrace the opportunity for self-reflection: George's long walk home allows him time to reflect on his life and the challenges he is facing. Sometimes, taking a step back and analyzing our situation can lead to valuable insights and personal growth.

2. Recognize the impact of negativity: George's wife's ultimatum highlights the destructive power of negativity in relationships. Negativity not only affects our own well-being but also impacts those around us. Being aware of our negative tendencies and striving to change them can lead to healthier and happier relationships.

3. Seek help and ask for support: George's plea for help to the universe demonstrates the importance of reaching out for assistance during difficult times. Our difficulties don't have to be faced by us alone. Seeking help from others, whether it's friends, family, or professionals, can provide guidance, support, and a fresh perspective.

Self-reflection Questions

1. Have you taken the time to step back and reflect on your life and the challenges you're facing?

2. How aware are you of the impact your negativity may have on your relationships and those around you?

Chapter 4 - George Wakes Up

Key Lessons

1. Accepting personal responsibility: George realizes that he is the one facing challenges in his life and it is up to him to turn things around. Taking ownership of one's situation is the first step towards positive change.

2. Confronting reality: George confronts the harsh reality of his failing marriage, potential job loss, and the need to improve himself. Acknowledging the truth, no matter how uncomfortable, is essential for growth and transformation.

3. The power of self-reflection: Through self-reflection, George gains clarity about his own role in his struggles. By looking inward and examining his choices and actions, he begins to understand the changes he needs to make to create a better future.

Self-reflection Questions

1. Have you accepted personal responsibility for the challenges you face in your life?

2. Have you confronted the reality of your current situation and acknowledged the need for positive change?

Chapter 5 - No Joy on the Bus

Key Lessons

1. Don't let negativity consume you: George realizes that constantly hearing negative comments from others can be overwhelming. It's important not to let the negativity define your self-worth and drag you down.

2. Appreciate kindness and empathy: George regrets being rude to Joy, the bus driver, who was genuinely trying to be nice to him. This chapter highlights the importance of recognizing and appreciating acts of kindness and empathy from others.

3. Take responsibility for your life: George acknowledges that changes need to happen quickly in his life, and he realizes that he must take the initiative to save his job, family, and marriage. This chapter emphasizes the importance of taking ownership and actively working towards positive change in your own life.

Self-reflection Questions

1. How can you prevent negativity from consuming your thoughts and affecting your self-esteem?

2. Are you taking the time to appreciate acts of kindness and empathy from others in your life?

Chapter 6 - The Rules

Key Lessons

1. Embrace the Power of Positive Energy: The Energy Bus is all about positive energy, and it plays a crucial role in transforming your life, work, and team. By embracing positivity and radiating it, you can create a more uplifting and productive environment.

2. Stay Open and Receptive to Change: Never turn your back on something that has the potential to change your life forever. Being open to new experiences, ideas, and perspectives allows you to grow personally and professionally. Recognize change as an opportunity for growth and improvement.

3. Don't Underestimate the Importance of Rules: Rules may sometimes seem restrictive, but they can provide valuable guidance and structure. The 10 rules on The Energy Bus are designed to fuel your life with positive energy and help you navigate challenges. Embrace these rules as tools for personal and professional transformation.

Self-reflection Questions

1. How can you actively incorporate positive energy into your daily life, work, and interactions with others?

2. Are you open and receptive to change, and do you view it as an opportunity for growth and improvement?

Chapter 7 - You're the Driver

Key Lessons

1. Take responsibility for your life: Recognize that you are the driver of your own life. Embrace the fact that you have the power to choose the direction you want to go and take control of your bus.

2. Seek guidance, but make your own decisions: While it's essential to seek advice and directions from others, ultimately, the decisions you make should align with your goals and desires. Don't let others dictate the course of your life.

3. Embrace the power of choice: Understand that choice is your greatest gift. Choose your attitude, choose your energy, and choose the vision for your life. Your choices shape your experience and determine the quality of your journey.

Self-reflection Questions

1. Are you taking responsibility for your life and actively driving towards your desired destination?

2. How are you exercising your power of choice to shape your attitude, energy, and vision for your life?

Chapter 8 - It's All About Energy

Key Lessons

1. Everything in our lives, including our thoughts, actions, and relationships, is fueled by energy. Understanding and harnessing this energy is crucial for creating a fulfilling and successful life.

2. The energy we surround ourselves with greatly impacts our well-being and success. Surrounding ourselves with positive, uplifting people and engaging in activities that energize us can lead to greater happiness and productivity.

3. Developing a clear vision for our lives and consistently focusing our energy towards that vision is essential for achieving our goals. By setting clear intentions and aligning our actions with our vision, we can mobilize the energy needed to create the life we desire.

Self-reflection Questions

1. Are you aware of the energy you surround yourself with and how it affects your well-being and success?

2. Have you defined a clear vision for your life and work, and are you actively directing your energy towards that vision?

Chapter 9 - George Shares His Vision

Key Lessons

1. Reflect on what you truly want: George realizes the importance of taking time to think about his personal vision and desires. By reflecting on what he wants for his life, he begins to rediscover his passions and sets goals for his physical and emotional well-being.

2. Build positive relationships: George expresses his vision for a stronger marriage, highlighting the significance of nurturing a positive relationship with his wife. He aims to create moments of laughter and rekindle the love they once shared, emphasizing the importance of investing in meaningful connections with loved ones.

3. Embrace crises as opportunities: Joy explains that crises can serve as turning points for growth and positive change. George's current challenges with his career and team become an opportunity for him to step up, motivate his colleagues, and lead them toward a successful product launch. By embracing the crisis, George can transform it into a catalyst for personal and professional development.

Self-reflection Questions

1. Have you taken the time to reflect on what you truly want for your life? What goals and desires do you want to pursue?

2. Are you embracing crises and challenges as opportunities for growth and positive change? How can you use difficult situations to develop yourself and create better outcomes?

Chapter 10 - Focus

Key Lessons

1. Focus on your vision: Spending time thinking about what you want rather than what you don't want helps attract positive outcomes and opportunities.

2. Avoid complaining and negativity: Complaining only brings more things to complain about and prevents you from creating what you truly desire. Shift your energy towards positivity.

3. Visualization enhances performance: Olympic athletes use visualization to improve their performance, and you can apply the same technique to create a successful and fulfilling life. See yourself achieving your goals and take action towards them.

Self-reflection Questions

1. Are you spending enough time focusing on your vision and what you want to achieve?

2. Are you actively avoiding complaining and negativity, and instead channeling your energy towards positivity and creating what you desire?

Chapter 11 - The Power of Positive Energy

Key Lessons

1. Positive energy is essential for creating success: Positive energy is like high octane fuel for your journey in life. It helps you overcome obstacles, stay focused, and inspire others. Cultivate positive thoughts, feelings, and actions to keep your ride moving forward.

2. Release negativity and focus on gratitude: When faced with negative situations, consciously let go of the negativity. Instead, choose to be grateful for what you have and appreciate the positive aspects of your life. Where there is a negative, there is always a positive.

3. Fuel up daily with positive thoughts, feelings, and actions: To maintain positive energy, it's crucial to actively fuel up each day. Fill your mind with positive thoughts, cultivate positive emotions, and take positive actions. By doing so, you prevent negativity from taking over and keep your ride on track.

Self-reflection Questions

1. Are you actively fueling up with positive thoughts, feelings, and actions each day to keep your energy levels high?

2. How can you release negativity and focus on gratitude in challenging situations to maintain a positive outlook?

Chapter 12 - George Takes a Walk

Key Lessons

1. Gratitude and physical activity can boost positive energy: George's Thank-You Walk combining gratitude and walking demonstrates the power of being grateful and active to energize the body and mind.

2. Positive emotions fuel productivity: After his walk, George feels more positive, energized, and ready to tackle his work. This highlights the link between positive emotions and increased productivity in the workplace.

3. Choosing positivity over appearances: George reflects on the example of his friend Chuck, realizing that appearances can be deceiving. He learns the importance of prioritizing inner happiness and positive energy over external success and possessions.

Self-reflection Questions

1. How can you incorporate gratitude and physical activity into your daily routine to boost your positive energy levels?

2. Are you prioritizing external appearances or inner happiness and positive energy in your life and work? What changes can you make to align your focus with a more positive and fulfilling path?

Chapter 13 - One Great Golf Shot Theory

Key Lessons

1. Focus on the positive: Instead of dwelling on the bad shots in life, focus on the one great thing that happened each day. This mindset will inspire you to create more success in the future.

2. Find inspiration in your successes: Just like a golfer remembers and cherishes their best shot, reflect on your accomplishments and successes. Let the feeling of these moments drive you to keep striving for more.

3. Share the power of positive energy: Spread the one great golf shot theory with others, particularly those who tend to focus on the negative. Encourage them to shift their mindset and find inspiration in their daily successes, fueling their own positive energy.

Self-reflection Questions

1. Are you focusing on the positive aspects of your day and finding inspiration in your successes?

2. Have you shared the one great golf shot theory with others who could benefit from shifting their mindset and finding inspiration in their own daily successes?

Chapter 14 - Bus Tickets

Key Lessons

1. Inviting others on your journey: Bus tickets serve as a powerful tool to invite people onto your bus and share your vision for the road ahead. By clearly communicating your goals and expectations, you can rally others to join you in achieving success.

2. Sharing your vision: It is essential to share your vision with your team and loved ones. By explaining where you want to go and how you plan to get there, you inspire others to align themselves with your goals and work together towards a common objective.

3. Communication is key: Clear and effective communication is crucial when inviting others onto your bus. Articulate your expectations, emphasize collaboration over personal egos, and convey the importance of everyone coming together for a shared purpose.

Self-reflection Questions

1. Have you clearly communicated your vision for the road ahead to those you want to invite on your journey?

2. Are you effectively conveying your expectations and emphasizing the collective importance of working together towards a shared goal?

Chapter 15 - A Very Long Weekend

Key Lessons

1. Embrace the power of patience: Like Abraham Lincoln waiting for battle reports, sometimes we have to be patient and wait for our fate to unfold. Use the weekend as a time to practice patience and trust that things will work out in due time.

2. Reflect and recharge: Use the long weekend as an opportunity to reflect on your journey and recharge your energy. Take this time to assess your progress, reevaluate your goals, and ensure you're on the right path.

3. Maintain a positive mindset: Regardless of the challenges or uncertainties ahead, choose to maintain a positive mindset during the long weekend. Focus on positive thoughts, affirmations, and activities that uplift your spirit and set the tone for a successful week ahead.

Self-reflection Questions

1. How can you embrace patience during a long weekend to trust that things will work out in due time?

2. What positive activities and thoughts can you engage in during the long weekend to recharge your energy and maintain a positive mindset for the upcoming week?

Chapter 16 - Who's on the Bus

Key Lessons

1. Choose your passengers wisely: Surround yourself with positive, supportive individuals who believe in your vision and are willing to contribute to the success of the team. Avoid negative influences that can bring down the energy and hinder progress.

2. Recognize the impact of team dynamics: Understand that the dynamics within your team can greatly influence its success. Address conflicts and negative attitudes promptly to prevent them from spreading and disrupting the overall energy and productivity.

3. Stay focused on the destination: Despite encountering setbacks and facing individuals who doubt your goals, remain focused on your vision and objectives. Keep moving forward with determination and inspire others to share your positive energy and commitment to success.

Self-reflection Questions

1. Are you intentionally surrounding yourself with positive and supportive individuals who contribute to your success?

2. How effectively are you managing team dynamics to ensure a positive and productive energy within your team?

Chapter 17 - The Enemy Is Negativity

Key Lessons

1. Negativity is pervasive: Negativity will always be present in various forms, whether it's negative people, self-doubt, or fear. Recognize that negativity is an ever-present enemy that can drain your energy and hinder your success.

2. Don't take negativity personally: When faced with negative people or situations, don't internalize it as a personal attack. Step back and understand that negativity is not about you; it's a reflection of the other person's mindset or circumstances.

3. Preserve your energy: Don't waste your valuable energy on those who don't support or believe in you. Focus on the people who are on your side and willing to contribute positively. By conserving your energy, you can invest it in driving your own bus and attracting like-minded individuals.

Self-reflection Questions

1. How can you recognize and navigate the presence of negativity in your life without taking it personally?

2. How can you prioritize and conserve your energy by focusing on the people who support and contribute positively to your goals?

Chapter 18 - No Energy Vampires on the Bus

Key Lessons:

1. Surround yourself with a positive support team: Your success and life are influenced by the people you surround yourself with. Be selective and surround yourself with individuals who increase your energy and support your goals and vision.

2. Identify and eliminate energy vampires: Energy vampires are people who drain your energy and hinder your success. Post a sign that says "NO ENERGY VAMPIRES ALLOWED" on your bus and be strong enough to remove negativity from your life and team.

3. Give people a chance, but set boundaries: Provide an opportunity for negative individuals to change, but if they continue to hinder your progress, be willing to take action and remove them from your bus. Create a positive and supportive environment where negativity is not tolerated.

.

Self-reflection Questions

1. Are you surrounding yourself with a positive support team that uplifts and supports your goals and vision?

2. Have you identified any energy vampires in your life or team, and are you taking decisive action to remove negativity and create a positive environment?

Chapter 19 - The Ultimate Rule of Positive Energy

Key Lessons

1. Positive energy and vision must exceed negativity: Your positive energy and vision should be stronger than anyone else's negativity, doubts, and skepticism. By maintaining unwavering certainty in your vision, you can overcome obstacles and inspire others.

2. Develop inner strength to combat negativity: Cultivate your positive energy as a habit, just like building a muscle. Repetition and focus on positive energy will make it your natural state. Strengthen yourself to respond to negativity with resilience and optimism.

3. Find value within yourself and others: Discover the inherent worth and potential within yourself and the people around you. Recognizing and nurturing this value creates a positive impact on your life, the lives of others, and the success of your team.

Self-reflection Questions

1. How can you ensure that your positive energy and vision remain stronger than any negativity or doubts you encounter?

2. What steps can you take to develop the inner strength necessary to overcome negativity and respond with resilience and optimism?

Chapter 20 - George Takes Control of His Bus

Key Lessons

1. Stand up against negativity: George learns the importance of confronting negativity and taking decisive action to remove it from his team. By setting clear expectations and not tolerating negative influences, he creates a more positive environment.

2. Believe in yourself: George realizes that the lack of belief in himself was contributing to his team's lack of faith in him as a leader. He learns the significance of valuing himself and gaining confidence, which empowers him to make difficult decisions and assert control over his bus.

3. Build a united team: George understands that having a team moving in the same direction and working towards common goals is more important than individual talent. He prioritizes team cohesion and a positive mindset over individual skill, which ultimately leads to a stronger and more productive team.

Self-reflection Questions

1. Are you taking ownership of your leadership role and actively shaping the direction of your team?

2. Are you standing up against negativity and creating a positive environment for your team to thrive?

Chapter 21 - George Has a Dream

Key Lessons

1. Embrace trust: George's dream taught him to trust that great things are happening, even in the face of uncertainty. Trusting the process and having faith can lead to positive outcomes.

2. Find peace in chaos: Despite the bus hurtling towards destruction, George experiences a sense of peace when he trusts in the greater plan. It highlights the importance of finding inner peace amidst chaotic situations.

3. Adapt to surprises: Life can change unexpectedly, and George learns to adapt and embrace surprises. Being open to new possibilities and adjusting to unforeseen circumstances can lead to positive transformations.

Self-reflection Questions

1. How can you cultivate trust in the midst of uncertainty to believe that great things are happening?

2. How can you find inner peace and maintain a calm mindset during chaotic situations in your life?

Chapter 22 - Better Today than Yesterday

Key Lessons

1. Embrace continuous improvement: Strive to be better today than you were yesterday. Focus on personal growth, learning from mistakes, and building upon successes. Instead of outperforming others, the objective is to better oneself.

2. Take ownership of your development: Recognize that the responsibility for becoming a better leader, person, spouse, or parent lies with you. Actively seek opportunities for growth, invest in self-improvement, and commit to making positive changes.

3. Foster a culture of improvement: Encourage your team to embrace the mindset of continuous improvement. Inspire them to strive for personal and collective growth, support their development, and create an environment where everyone feels motivated to improve and succeed.

Self-reflection Questions

1. Are you actively seeking opportunities to improve yourself and grow, both personally and professionally?

2. How can you foster a culture of continuous improvement within your team or organization?

Self-assessment Questions

Chapter 1 - Flat Tire:

- How does a flat tire impact your journey?
- What can you do to overcome unexpected obstacles?

Chapter 2 - Good News and Bad News:

- How can good news positively affect your mindset?
- How can you turn bad news into an opportunity?

Chapter 3 - The Long Walk Home:

- What lessons can you learn from a challenging situation?
- How can you stay motivated during a difficult journey?

Chapter 4 - George Wakes Up:

- Why is self-awareness important for personal growth?
- How can you start your day with a positive mindset?

Chapter 5 - No Joy on the Bus:

- What happens when negativity dominates your environment?
- How can you spread joy and positivity to others?

Chapter 6 - The Rules:

- What are the benefits of establishing personal rules?
- How can you create rules that align with your values?

Chapter 7 - You're the Driver:

- How does taking responsibility for your life empower you?
- What actions can you take to steer your life in the right direction?

Chapter 8 - It's All About Energy:

- Why is energy essential for success and well-being?
- How can you manage and increase your energy levels?

Chapter 9 - George Shares His Vision:

- What makes having a clear vision so crucial?

- How can you communicate your vision effectively to others?

Chapter 10 - Focus:

- How does focusing on your goals contribute to your success?
- What strategies can you use to maintain focus?

Chapter 11 - The Power of Positive Energy:

- What impact does positive energy have on your relationships?
- How can you cultivate and radiate positive energy?

Chapter 12 - George Takes a Walk:

- Why is taking time for yourself crucial for personal growth?
- How can walking or being in nature enhance your well-being?

Chapter 13 - One Great Golf Shot Theory:

- What can you learn from a successful moment in your life?
- How can you apply the concept of "one great shot" to other areas?

Chapter 14 - Bus Tickets:

- What are the consequences of negative people in your life?
- How can you choose who gets a "ticket" on your bus?

Chapter 15 - A Very Long Weekend:

- How can you make the most of your weekends or leisure time?
- What activities or habits can rejuvenate your energy?

Chapter 16 - Who's on the Bus:

- Who are the people you surround yourself with, and why does it matter?
- How can you evaluate and choose the right people to be on your bus?

Chapter 17 - The Enemy Is Negativity:

- How does negativity impact your mindset and overall well-being?
- What strategies can you use to combat negativity?

Chapter 18 - No Energy Vampires on the Bus:

- What are energy vampires, and why should you avoid them?
- How can you protect yourself from the draining effects of energy vampires?

Chapter 19 - The Ultimate Rule of Positive Energy:

- What is the ultimate rule of positive energy, and why is it important?
- How can you apply this rule to fuel your life and interactions?

Chapter 20 - George Takes Control of His Bus:
- How can you take control of your life and make positive changes?
- What steps can you take to create a more positive and fulfilling journey?

Chapter 21 - George Has a Dream:
- Why is having a dream or vision important for your success?
- How can you pursue and manifest your dreams?

Chapter 22 - Better Today than Yesterday:
- How can you strive to be better each day?
- What actions can you take to continuously improve yourself and your life?

Made in United States
Troutdale, OR
02/13/2024

17643295R00046